Words from the Pew

by Charles E. Martin

To: DEO Gilbert
My Gou Continue to Lead
Your Heard. Take the youth
Forth.
Charles Martin

DORRANCE
PUBLISHING CO
EST. 1920
PITTSBURGH, PENNSYLVANIA 15222

Dorrance Publishing Co
701 Smithfield Street
Pittsburgh, PA 15222
Visit our website at *www.dorrancebookstore.com*

ISBN: 978-1-4809-1098-0
eISBN 978-1-4809-1420-9

Acknowledgments

Material taken from God's Best Secrets by Andrew Murray. Copyright©
1998 by Whitaker House. Use by permission of Whitaker House.

Quotes taken from *My Utmost for His Highest* by Oswald Chamber, ©
1935 by Dodd Mead & Co., renewed © 1963 by the Oswald Chambers
Publications Assn., Ltd. Used by permission of Discovery House Publishing, Grand Rapids MI 49501. All rights reserved.

All Bible Scriptures if not so indicated are from the Holy Bible, New International Version ®, NIV® Copyright © 1973, 1978, 1984 by Biblica,
Inc.® Used by permission. All rights reserved worldwide.

Spurgeon's Commentary on Greatest Chapters of the Bible Copyright ©
1998 Thomas Carter. Published by Kregel Publications, Grand Rapids, MI.
Used by permission of the publisher. All rights reserved.

Scripture from the Holy Bible, King James Version Copyright © 1989
Thomas Nelson, Inc. Used by permission. All rights reserved.

Quotes taken from the Commentary on the Whole Bible by Matthew Henry,
Copyright ©1961 by Zondervan Publishing House. Used by permission of
Zondervan Publishing House.

Quotes from The Treasury of Religious & Spiritual Quotations Copyright
© 1994 The Stonesong Press, Inc., used by permission. All rights reserved.

The Life Application Study Bible, New International Version, Copyright
© 1988. 1989, 1990, 1991, 2005, bonded version by Zondervan Publishing
House. Used by permission. All rights reserved.

Liberty Commentary Copyright © 1982 by Old-Time Gospel Hour; All
rights reserved under International and Pan-American Conventions; Published in Nashville, Tennessee, by Thomas Nelson, Inc.

Quotes from Jesus Calling, Copyright © 2004 Sarah Young, Used by Permission of Harper Collins, Inc. All rights reserved.

Introduction

I never knew where these writings would lead me when they started. God gave me this assignment when I was teaching Sunday school. My intention was simply to provide additional biblical information to those in attendance. It turned out this was not the right setting for these writings. However, I knew I could not let that stop me from writing what God placed in my head and my heart. It had to come out. So I continued to write with the idea that someday it would become a book. The writings herein are the words the Holy Spirit placed in my heart and I believe they serve a divine purpose. Spurgeon says, "Let us be willing to follow wherever our Lord calls us. Whether it be to service or suffering, if he leads the way, we can follow." I do believe the will of God was done in my writing this book. I give praise to the Father for the leading of the Holy Spirit and enabling me to complete this work.

I would like to thank my wife, Betty, and my sister, Mildred Johnson, for their patience with me during this endeavor and their help in reading my manuscript and suggestions.

I would like to dedicate this book to my mother, Dorothy Martin whom I love dearly, for her continued prayers. The answering of her prayers were inspirational in leading me to finding a church home, growing in the word of God and the writing of this book.

Contents

John versus John

John versus John does not appear to be a topic of biblical proportions. When we think of the word "versus," what comes to mind? Someone being against someone else, as in a legal case, a fight between two opponents, or even two opposing sides on an issue all come into one's thinking. However, I am here to tell you that this is not the case. In fact, this subject really means just the opposite and could maybe be entitled as John confirms John or even John Reiterates his Previous Teaching. Now, how did I arrive at this conclusion? In my morning devotional reading, my initial interpretation of a passage lead me to think that I was reading something when in fact I was actually in a different book of the Bible altogether. At this time I had to take a look at the actual passage of scripture I had in mind, and I came to the conclusion that John versus John was a subject to be addressed. This may not be the case for all, and many have probably looked at this subject in the past. But for me, it was an "aha" moment. God had revealed something to me, and I needed to delve for the greater meaning.

John versus John is really an understanding of two passages from two books of John, John of the Gospels and 1st John. The Gospel of John revealed that John believed that Jesus Christ was the Son of God and that all who believe in Him will have eternal life. On the other hand, 1st John was written to reassure Christians in their faith and to counter false teachings. Here are two different perspectives with different meanings. However, if we look a little closer, we can deduce something divinely arranged in John's writings.

John 1: 1-4 of the NIV reads: "In the beginning was the Word, and the Word was with God, and the Word was God. He was with God in the beginning.

Through Him all things were made; without Him nothing was made that has been made. In Him was life, and that life was the light of men." How do I approach this passage in scripture? Here John attempts to show that Jesus Christ is the Son of God, one with the Father.

The Word, of whom he speaks, is operative in verse 1. John closes his discourse on God, the Word, becoming Human with verse 18: "No one has ever seen God, but God the One and Only Son, who is at the Father's side, has made Him known." We know from the Bible that Jesus is the one at the Father's side. These verses of scripture can be hard for non-Christians to understand, but I will try to give a short version. To gain fuller understanding of these verses we should note that Word is two-fold. One is the word conceived, and the other is word uttered. Matthew Henry explains the word conceived as "thought, which is the first and only immediate product and conception of the soul." Therefore the second person in the Trinity, Jesus Christ, is the Word conceived or the Word thought. Let's now use the Word uttered to tie this together. The Word uttered is the speech that comes out of our mouth. When the Word was spoken, it left the thought process and became verbal, or something placed into being, which we can identify with because it now has life. By proper substitution, in the beginning was the Word and the Word was with God, and The Word was God and He was with God in the beginning, then when the word became spoken or verbal we have Jesus Christ as a being. This speaks to the existence of Christ not only before His incarnation, but before all time. He was spirit before He became man as God is Spirit, as John asserts in 4:24.

The next operative word we want to explore is "made," mentioned three times in verse 3. This verse shows the active participation of Jesus Christ in all that was made. He had divine existence in the beginning of time. Through Him all things were made, making Him part of all that God the Father did and proving that He is God.

Verse 4 identified Him as life and in Him was the light of men. We know from Genesis 2:7 that God breathed the breath of life into man's nostrils. If everything was done through Jesus, then He was a participant in this action. Not only does Jesus have life in Himself, but He is the true God and the living God. All that has life, creatures or man, have life through Him. Life in man is far greater than it is in creatures. It is sound judgment based on scripture. In Him was also the light of men. The spirit of man is the light or candle of the Lord burning inside us. It is this spirit, upon accepting Jesus Christ as our Lord and Savior, that allows divine revelation to enter into our mind and heart through the Word of God.

Having focused on John 1: 1-4, now let's focus on 1ˢᵗ John 1: 1-3. NIV translation is as follows:

> *That which was from the beginning, which we have heard, which we have seen with our eyes, which we have looked at and our hands have touched – this we proclaim concerning the Word of life. The life appeared, we have seen it and testify to it, and we proclaim to you the eternal life, which was with the father and has appeared to us. We proclaim to you what we have seen and heard, so that you also may have fellowship with us. And our fellowship is with the Father and with his Son, Jesus Christ.*

We previously surmised that 1ˢᵗ John was written to reassure Christians in their faith and to counter false teachings. How does this have anything to do with the Gospel of John 1:1-4? A closer look at the passage reference should reveal some points of mutual understanding. Once again I arrived at this conclusion because I thought I was reading something that I really was not reading, or my mind was leading me in that direction when in fact it was in a different book of the Bible altogether.

That which was from the beginning has a familiar ring to John 1:1. The difference is that in the Gospel we understand that the Word was Christ who existed before the creation. Now Christ has been manifested in the flesh and John is addressing the issue from a different perspective of that which was from the beginning. We now have the Word as verbal, or something placed into being which we can identify with, because it has been spoken. Now we have a living body that the apostle has heard, seen with his own eyes, and touched. This is an introduction of the eternal Word of Life, Jesus the Christ, that was with the eternal Father, God from the beginning.

In 1ˢᵗ John, we have the evidence of what was written in John 1: 1-4. His heavenly or divine explanation has now turned to realization. The Word is no longer conceived but has assumed a mouth and tongue, that he might utter words of life. The utterance this time was a creation of a different kind. The words uttered have the ring of from the beginning but start with belief and acceptance of The Word, Jesus Christ as our Lord and Savior through the evidence given. The words in the beginning uttered this time also meant the beginning of the Church of Jesus Christ.

It is here spoken of hearing, seeing and touching. The senses are receptors of the mind. When used to work for the cause of Jesus or the Church, John uses them as his reference for witnessing for Christ. His senses enabled him to see Christ for who he was in real life and witness to other Christians. It was the duty of John and the other Apostles to share the evidence by which they were led, when the Holy Spirit descended upon them during Pentecost. By doing so, the disciples could rest in the Peace of Christ and have full confidence in the institution of the Church which they embraced.

Their faith and loyalty to our Savior resulted in fellowship among the saints. Fellowship on this side with saints through following the Word of God leads to fellowship on the other side in eternity with God and our Lord and Savior, Jesus the Christ.

In this comparison of John versus John, we see the revealing of divine knowledge. The Holy Spirit allowed John to use two somewhat similar passages in scripture to explain two vastly different concepts. The same Holy Spirit that allowed John to do this is available to us. Our continued studying of God's word will allow us to hear His voice as He reveals different interpretation of scripture. This is simply the receipt of divine knowledge through the continued application and study of God's word. The more we avail ourselves to Him, the more He allows us to understand. Our knowledge is limited, and the secrets of God will not be revealed to us unless we open our minds and heart to receive His blessings.

So with me, John versus John started with "in the beginning". In the beginning was when I sat down on this day to do my daily devotional; I had a divine appointment. That appointment was with God and the word He placed in my heart. It is my prayer that He continues to speak to me and allow me to share His word with others.

Have You Been Chosen

To believe in our Lord and Savior Jesus the Christ is worth far more than its weight in gold. It not only identifies you as a believer but describes the person you have chosen to become. To be chosen goes beyond our choosing to accept Jesus as our Lord and Savior. It means that we have joined a privileged group of people, a royal family: The Church of our Lord and Savior, Jesus the Christ.

The Twelve Apostles were chosen by Jesus. They were fishermen, a tax collector, and other occupations not identified in the Bible. Simon the Zealot, a member of a Jewish Patriotic Party, who resisted Roman aggression, was so called to distinguish him from Simon Peter. We do not know the process for choosing these twelve, with the exception that they were chosen and had a place in the life and ministry of Jesus and would be receivers of The Great Commission.

Eventually, they would be sent out to preach the Gospel, as this was part of God's plan for man. Judas Iscariot, the disciple who is known as the betrayer of Jesus did not receive this honor. In fact, after his betrayal of Jesus, he grieved because of his actions and committed suicide. However, they all had one thing in common: they were chosen. The choosing of Judas Iscariot was vital to the fulfillment of Old Testament prophecy.

Actually, they were all chosen by God in the person of Jesus, the Son of Man. There was the choosing of another twelfth Apostle, Matthias. This is identified in Acts 1:26. Peter in Acts 1:20 cited Psalms 69:25 and 109:8 as reason for choosing a replacement for Judas. In these Psalms I find reason for replacement of one in a leadership position, but I cannot connect the prophecy of choosing a replacement for Judas as a Messianic Vision by

David referring to the betrayal of Jesus. Matthias is a sound choice. He is chosen because he was a disciple who had been among them from John's baptism of Jesus through the time when Jesus was taken away. This is noteworthy since many fell away because they did not believe Jesus was from Heaven. He was man's choosing as an Apostle. However, John 6:44 exclaims, "No one can come to me unless the Father who sent me draws him," and verse 65, which reads, "This is why I told you that no one can come to me unless the Father has enabled him." He was chosen as a follower because the Father handpicked him.

Paul's conversion came on the Damascus Road, where he was chosen by Jesus to go forth and preach the Gospel. His choosing was confirmed in Acts 9 when, in verse 15, Jesus told Ananias, "Go! This man is my chosen instrument to carry my name before the Gentiles, and their kings and before the people of Israel." He was chosen by Jesus to be an Apostle.

Have you been chosen? Do you believe that Jesus is the Son of God and have accepted Him as your Lord and Savior? If you truly have done this, then you are chosen. If you have not, it is never too late. However, this is not the end of the story. Since we have free will, it is easy for Satan to place road blocks in our path. To reach eternal life with Christ we must have faith in the Word of God, do our very best to live by these words, and follow the path Jesus laid for all His followers. If we do these things, then the words of Jesus such as John 6:37, "All that the Father gives me will come to me, and whoever comes to me I will never drive away," and 17:24, "Father, I want those you have given me to be with me where I am, and to see my glory, the glory you have given me because you loved me before the creation of the world," will lead to eternal life. As Christians we must realize that Jesus does not work independently of God but with Him for the greater glory of God, reconciling sinners to Him, for we are all born into a world of sin.

In the first paragraph I said, "It means that we have joined a privileged group of people, a royal family." Now we realize that the choosing by God is essential and to maintain that membership is incumbent upon each believer.

What am I Willing to Do for God

Philippians 1:20 reads, "I eagerly expect and hope that I will in no way be ashamed, but will have sufficient courage so that now as always Christ will be exalted in my body, whether by life or by death."

Oswald Chambers writes, "To get there is a question of will, not of debate nor of reasoning, but a surrender of will, an absolute and irrevocable surrender on that point."

The Life Application Study Bible says, "If you're not ready to die, then you're not ready to live. Make certain of your eternal destiny; then you will be free to serve – devoting your life to what really counts, without fear of death."

Do not be ashamed of your Lord and Savior. Paul wants to continue his work for our Lord and Savior Jesus Christ. However, here lies a problem that a lot of Christians have. Can I actively work for God without being ashamed of Him? Am I willing to relay God's word no matter what the cost? In order to do this, I must be willing to stand tall and not be ashamed of what the Spirit leads me to say or do. If I live for Christ I will accomplish the will of God. Can I do this?

Amos 6:10 surmises that people were afraid to mention the Lord's name because they had failed to call upon the name of the Lord for salvation. We should be bold in the use of the name of God and our Lord and Savior Jesus Christ. If God's word has really manifested itself in our hearts, then we will be willing to stand for Him at all times. Even in bad times and in bad health, we should know that God is God and His Word is true. Therefore, we should never be ashamed to speak His name and give Him all the praise and glory He deserves. As we grow as Christians and learn to reverence the Lord, the use of His name and words becomes easier and easier and our identification with Him will be evidenced in our lives daily. I will not be ashamed of my Lord and Savior.

We must yield to God and ask for the help we need. We are not strong enough on our own.

He (Paul) in essence asks for sufficient courage so that Christ would always be exalted in his body. Paul had learned that the assignment Jesus gave him was a task with several layers of responsibility. With each step, his task seemed even harder. He knew that he had to have a sufficiency of courage so that Christ would be exalted in him. Having studied under one of the chief Jewish rabbis, or teachers, Gamaliel, he was well versed in the writings of the prophets. We can then assume that Isaiah's writings were embedded in his memory and that he realized that God was all sufficient. He would remember what God told Jeremiah, "that He was the God of all mankind and that nothing was too hard for Him." After receiving his orders from Jesus, knowing the sufficiency that rests in God and realizing nothing is too hard for God, Paul realized he could run the race Jesus set before him. He realized that God would meet all his needs according to his glorious riches in Christ Jesus (Philippians 4:19). He thus realized that Jesus had given him everything he needed for life and godliness when he called him to the task. There is sufficiency in Christ; therefore there is sufficient courage in us when we trust in the Lord.

Paul realized that he had been called by Jesus as an Apostle to the Gentiles. He lived his life, after his calling by Jesus, according to the Word of God and had no regrets for what he had done or would do for Jesus. To die, for Paul, was to leave the life he once led as a Pharisee who studied under Gamaliel and to follow the path laid for him by Jesus. In doing so, he had a new understanding of God's word, what it meant to live for Jesus, and had realized his calling under the authority of Jesus as an Apostle to the Gentiles. In order to live for Jesus, we must be willing to part with those things in our lives that hinder our progression toward our eternal home, Heaven. Just as there were layers in Paul's journey, things he had to accomplish in order to further his cause, we have to strip away the layers in our lives that prevent us from living totally for Jesus. As we do this, we begin to live the life God created us for. We become thankful for each day realizing that it is a step on the path of righteousness and openly give God all the praise and glory.

Am I prepared to give my life to Him and do His will? What am I willing to do for God? Am I ready to enjoy life and please Jesus by doing His will and die (give up all that is not Christlike to the best of my ability) because of His love for me and all that God has done for me and the realization that when death really does come, I can rest, not because I'm tired or my body is weary, but because I have run a good race. Whether by life or by death, I must be willing to do what God asks of me, and that is to carry the word that Jesus preached.

Take this Cup

I have often heard pastors and others say it isn't hard to follow the will of God. As I thought about this statement, the Holy Spirit immediately led me to the scripture of Jesus praying at Gethsemane prior to His betrayal and arrest. Thus the question arose: Take This Cup? Matthew, Mark and Luke all touch on this subject in their Gospel. Matthew looked at Jesus as the Messiah, the one who would deliver the Jews from Roman oppression. Mark viewed Jesus as a servant. He helped people by telling them about God, healing them, and ultimately giving His life for sin (the ultimate act of service). Luke, a doctor and historian, put great emphasis on dates and details enabling him to connect Jesus to events and people in history. No matter which way we look at it, this question of Take This Cup is of great significance and offers valuable substance for walking the Christian path.

Without taking a specific point of view from either of these Gospels, let us look at the question, "Take This Cup", from the perspective of Matthew 26:37-39 as the basis for this discussion.

> *He took Peter and the two sons of Zebedee along with him, and he began to be sorrowful and troubled. Then he said to them, "My soul is overwhelmed with sorrow to the point of death. Stay here and keep watch with me. Going a little farther, he fell to the ground and prayed. "My Father, if it is possible, may this cup be taken from me. Yet not as I will, but as you will.*

In these verses we have the story of Jesus' agony in the garden of Gethsemane. He took these three (Peter, James, and John) with him. Luke, as a doctor and historian, does not make mention of these apostles. It has been claimed that the reason he took these three is because they had witness of his glory in his transfiguration and that would prepare them to be the witness of his agony. This agony, or conflict, which he experienced was not bodily pain because it came from within. His heart was troubled because he carried a heavy weight upon his spirit. This agony can be attributed to his upcoming encounter with the powers of darkness, his awareness of the enormous weight of carrying the sins of the world upon his shoulders, and the suffering he would have to endure for this cause.

In response to this situation, Jesus did as he had often done on many occasions. He prayed to His Father. This prayer consisted of three sections which will help us to understand the question of "Take This Cup." First, he appealed to His Father; secondly, he made a request; and thirdly, he asked and answered his own question of "Yet not as I will, but as you will."

When we were children and even as adults, when things take a turn toward the worst, we often turn to our parents, if they are living, or remember the lessons they taught us before they departed. Jesus was no different. He had a problem of sorts, and he turned to the only one who could help him, his Father. Matthew Henry states, "A prayer of faith against affliction may very well consist with the patience of hope under affliction." Jesus knew that in his human strength he would not be able to face the future. However, with the strength of God his Father, he could withstand any combination of circumstances.

Secondly, in his request that this cup be taken from him, Jesus refers to his suffering as a cup. A cup can be defined as a small container or as one's portion, as of joy or suffering. These two definitions have something in common that we can easily identify with. A cup has a bottom, and its portion is only eight ounces. In other words, after eight ounces, it runs over or is given relief. So there is a limit to how much it can hold. One's portion of suffering is for only a little while. Psalm 30:5 NIV reads: "For his anger last only a moment but his favor last a lifetime; weeping may remain for a night, but rejoicing comes in the morning." Oh, what wonderful words of praise. Jesus knew his father was not angry with him because his mission was revealed prior to his taking on human form. He also knew that after completion of his mission he would sit at the right hand of the Father for eternity. But it gets even better. In his present situation, his weeping or agony can be described as the darkness he faced. But the joy, in the form of morning, would come in three days, and he would be raised to life never to die again. Well done, my good and faithful servant. Jesus, who came to serve, knew the rewards for good and faithful work unto his Father. We also see here the humanity of Jesus. He was not averse to pain and suffering.

And thirdly, "Yet not as I will, but as you will." Jesus knew full well what he would have to go through to save a dying world. The redemption and salvation of the world had been squarely placed on his shoulders. The reason for his submission was his obedience to his Father's will. Herman Melville writes in Moby Dick, "All the things that God would have us do are hard for us to do – remember that – and hence, He oftener commands us than endeavors to persuade. And if we obey God, we must disobey ourselves, wherein the hardness of obeying God consists." The question again arises, Take This Cup. Do we always do what Jesus did and deny our humanity?

Emil Brunner writes in The Divine Imperative, "Duty and genuine goodness are mutually exclusive….The sense of 'ought' shows me the Good at an infinite impassable distance from my will. Willing obedience is never the fruit of an 'ought' but only of love." Take This Cup? Our obedience to God stems from our Love from Him. Our Love for the Father enables us to endure more than we can ever imagine. The answer to the question, "If I Love God the way Christ loved his Father, I will endure and Take This Cup." becomes "I can do all things through Christ who strengthens me."

The Mystery of God's Word

"The Mystery of God's Word" is something we all know about as Christians. It has been debated by Dispensationalist and Covenant theologians as a way of comparing the spiritual conditions of the Old Testament believer and the New Testament Christian. I'm not a theologian, but I love "The Mystery of God's Word." I love reading God's word and, even more, writing about it when the Holy Spirit opens my heart and mind to pen my thoughts.

Psalm 16 is what gave me my introduction to this subject because it was described as a Michtam of David. Michtam is a word of uncertain meaning found in the titles of six psalms of David (16, 56-60). Some translate the word to mean "golden or precious." Others describes it as a poem or song found in the title of Psalm 16 and states it is rendered in the Septuagint (oldest Greek version of the Old Testament of the Bible) by a word meaning "tablet inscription." Putting all this together further helps me to understand that this Psalm is worth its weight in gold. It is fittingly titled in some books as A Messianic Psalm revealing the resurrection of Christ, but others do not share this same thought. This is a clear example of "The Mystery of God's Word." It speaks to different people in different ways.

While this Psalm does not speak wholeheartedly about the resurrection of Christ, I can see a manifestation of this revelation. I would not have seen this manifestation if it had not been for my fervent love of studying God's word during my daily devotional. For me, understanding of most of the Psalms does not readily avail itself and requires additional reading. My research zoned me in on verses 8-11 of the NIV translation:

> *I saw the Lord always before me. Because he is at my right*
> *hand, I will not be shaken. Therefore my heart is glad and*

my tongue rejoices; my body also will rest secure, because you will not abandon me to the grave, nor will you let your Holy One see decay. You have made known to me the path of life; you will fill me with joy in your presence, with eternal pleasures at your right hand.

In these verses I see two things at work: David's recognition of eternal life with God after he has left this world and the risen body of our Lord and Savior, Jesus the Christ. "I saw the Lord before me," as David speaks, can only refer to the heavenly presence of God. I see a risen Savior in the words "nor will you let your Holy One see decay," which has messianic overtones. We fully understand that when man dies he will not be raised from the dead until the second coming of Christ. Peter, in his addressing the crowd at Pentecost, restates the verses of this Psalm in Acts 2: 25-28. "The Mystery of God's Word" as here stated is elegantly described by Matthew Henry when he writes of this passage: "Something we may allow here of the workings of David's own pious and devout affection toward God … he carried the spirit of prophecy quite beyond the consideration of himself and his own case, to foretell the story of the Messiah."

It would be easy to continue this discussion of these verses in Psalm 16; however, it is not necessary. The one thing we must remember is in Isaiah 56:8-9, when he explained that God's thoughts are not our thoughts and God's thoughts are higher than our thoughts. Therefore God's thoughts or the "The Mystery of God's Word" can only be revealed to us by God Himself though His Holy Spirit as we read and study His word. Spend time in God's word daily, and he will reveal to you those heavenly things needed to continue your Christian walk and growth. "The Mystery of God's Word" is in us in the form of His Holy Spirit. We as Christians must give God His time in attendance at Church, Bible Study, Sunday school, and personal study to receive what we already have, His Word.

Am I Ready for His Coming

One thing that is for certain is, "Nobody knows the day or the hour," as explained to us in Matthew 24:36. Mark 13:33 says the same thing in a different way: "Be on guard! Be alert! You do not know when that time will come." These verses should alert us, as Christians, to be prepared for that day. In preparation for that day, we must realize that we may not be living when Christ returns. Therefore, our preparation should have already begun. In case you have not considered this, start your preparation today; it is never too late.

We prepare for temporal events all the time. In preparing for these events, we take great pride in the preparation, execution, and culmination of the planned event. We should feel this same way about the returning of our Lord and Savior Jesus the Christ.

There are ways to prepare for His coming. One of those ways can be attributed to the Gospel of Matthew, where he talks about the owner of the house and the thief. If the owner had known when the thief was coming, he would have been prepared. Since we do not know when Jesus is coming, we can prepare by keeping the Temple of God fit. Physical fitness is one thing, but spiritual fitness is another. Spiritual fitness is a must because we do not know when we will be called home to meet the Lord. We have the Holy Spirit to guide us. We should not lean to our own understanding but be led by the Holy Spirit and trust God to charter the path we should take. Psalm 119-105 reads, "Thy word is a lamp unto my feet, and a light unto my path." God's word is not designed to confound us but to reveal His truths and lead us on a path of growth and understanding of what he wills for our lives. Studying God's word is a way of strengthening us spiritually and added assurance for our fitness for entrance into the Kingdom of Heaven.

Stewardship is another area of spiritual fitness, and it involves the effective management of resources. Everything that we have is a gift from God. Our health, wealth, and abilities are all resources that God has allowed us to manage. We call on Him in times of need for replenishment, but the ultimate responsibility for proper usage of those resources belongs to us as Christians. Matthew uses The parable of Talents of Money (25:14-23) as an example of how the servants managed what their master had entrusted to them. The far country is the time between Jesus ascension into Heaven and His return. Those that managed the resources wisely were rewarded for their efforts. It is the same way with us. If we manage God's resources wisely, they become another feather in our hat. Using our time and gifts to work for the Lord is one way of managing those resources. Additionally, paying tithes is another way of managing those resources. Good stewardship is doing the best with what God has given each of us and increases our readiness for His coming.

We can't afford to give up or give out when it comes to preparing for the coming of Christ. Pray every day that God will allow you to be of benefit to someone, especially your Christian brothers and sisters. Study God's Word daily and pray that the Holy Spirit enjoins you in spiritual growth. Be good stewards and ask God to illuminate ways for you to use the resources He has entrusted to you. Am I ready for His Coming is a question we cannot wait to answer. If your preparation has not started, start today.

The Significance of the Tower of Babel

I received an e-mail today and a friend shared with me their learning about the Tower of Babel. I didn't think much about it at the time, but the subject remained on my mind. I could not sleep because of the understanding God revealed to me.

This person pointed our several areas in the passage. Now, the whole world had one language and a common speech. As men moved eastward, they found a plain in Shinar and settled there. They talked about making bricks and building a city. However, my friend's main attention was on how we came to have different languages as a people.

Their point is very interesting, but I think there is a much deeper meaning. The Life Application Study Bible explains it as the people building a monument to themselves to display their own greatness and a wonder for the world to see. It then goes on to say that building monuments to ourselves may not in itself be wrong, but when we use them to give identity and self-worth, they take God's place.

The Liberty Bible Commentary gives another interesting point. "Babel was certainly a special judgment on man's embodiment of the ungodly spirit that again characterized human civilization after the Flood. This is the cultural focus of mounting human arrogance."

Before reading these two explanations, my spirit led to another related meaning. During the Creation, God made man to serve Him and take care of His creation by giving him dominion over it. Serving and praising Him are the most important factors related to man in the Creation. We were created to serve God as He willed. There is only one way to know God's will, and that is through communication, better known as prayer for Christians.

The people of Babel had great communication skills with one problem. They only communicated among themselves. We were made to communicate with our Father, God in heaven. This communication is done through prayer guided by the Holy Spirit and transmitted to God through Jesus Christ as our great intercessor. God in His greatness, according to His will for our lives, releases the answer or blessing to our prayers, which are then relayed to Jesus Christ and made known to us through the Holy Spirit. This simple process, communication or prayer for Christians, shows the importance of the Holy Trinity in our lives. However, God may determine to make his wishes known to us in other ways. They may be through people or events.

The passage goes on to say, "And the Lord came down to see the city and the tower, which the children of men builded. And the Lord said, Behold, the people is one, and they have all one language: and this they begin to do: and now nothing will be restrained from them, which they have imagined to do" (KJV). In order to accomplish His divine will, God confused the language of the people, resulting in a language barrier and hindering the completion of their project. He also scattered them throughout the world because that was His will for the family of Noah, repopulation to all corners of the world.

In accomplishing these actions, God turned our focus, the focus of man, back to Him for fulfillment of our needs. "What man would not do willingly, God forced them to do as a result of judgment" (Liberty Bible Commentary). Sure, we have free will, but to accomplish the things that make our lives meaningful, we must comply with the will of God. May we remain connected to God through prayer and rely on His will for our lives to guide us safely during present times, leading us to a life of eternity with Him and our Lord and Savior in Heaven.

Freedom from Our Enemies

I arrived at this subject through many months of trying to identify the fifth freedom in Psalm 23. The Liberty Bible Commentary identifies four as: Freedom from want; Freedom from depletion; Freedom from the fear of evil or death; and Freedom from desertion. In my quest to identify the fifth freedom based on Psalm 23:5, "You prepare a table before me in the presence of my enemies. You anoint my head with oil; my cup overflows," my thinking by the guidance of the Holy Spirit lead me to "Freedom from Our Enemies" as the missing fifth freedom. "Freedom," as does "enemies," has many meanings. Freedom here deals with the spiritual aspects of this subject as exemption from external control or interference. Enemies, on the other hand, could be spirit or temporal (physical and mental).

This is not a far stretch of one's imagination. This passage of scripture contains three main components. The first, "You prepare a table before me in the presence of my enemies," is the key and easily explained. These words place us in the midst of God. Where could be safer than being in the arms of the Father.

When we come into the presence of God, enemies are always in tow because we leave the carnal and enter the spiritual. Satan follows us with the sole desire to steal, kill and destroy. People attack us, literally daily, from all sides with the sole purpose of physical or mental defeat. If we had to face our enemies alone, our weaknesses would show. Man's planning is not perfect. Even the greatest strategist cannot think of everything. However, when we put our trust in the Lord and let Him guide our way, His plans are failsafe. Psalm 138:7 reminds us that "Though I walk in the midst of trouble, you preserve my life. You stretch out your hand against the anger of my foes, with your right hand you save me." With His left hand we are cradled in His protection as if we were sitting at the table He has prepared for us, a place of tranquility in our temporal environment and peace in spiritual quietness.

The second part is "you anoint my head with oil." We came to the table with enemies in tow. Now the Lord had anointed our head with oil. This statement should touch the heart of every Christian. When we accepted Jesus Christ as our Lord and Savior, we were set apart and embarked on a path of dedicating our lives to the Creator, God. Metaphorically speaking, it could be very well said our heads were anointed with oil. In a since, we fall prostrate before the Lord, vowing to trust Him. We agreed to trust in His Word and follow His ways. On the basis of total trust, every moment of our life will be filled with the blessings of God. This is an intimate relationship. A relationship in which we not only read His Word daily for continued guidance but pray daily for new revelation. In doing so, we grow in all aspects of our relationship with God and become more like Christ. As a result, we receive spiritual freedom. We are also given discernment to avoid physical confrontations and guidance which increases our mental faculties in dealing with those things that are intangible, be they spiritual or temporal.

"My cup overflows" is another metaphor which exemplifies increase. This increase pervades all aspects of our Christian life. It is the additional grace God affords us, allowing us to walk in victory. Francois Fenelon wrote, in Spiritual Letters, "Grace only works effectively in us in proportion to our unremitting correspondence to it." Therefore, the more we commit ourselves to the will of God, the more grace we receive or protection because the light in us shines brighter. This grace also decreases the battles we fight because our faith has been strengthened. The strengthening of our faith through God's grace will not allow us to entertain thoughts of indifference to the will of God. The overflow becomes more apparent because we can realize the hand of God in the little things in life.

Why was this endeavor so important? Over the months I've read the 23rd Psalm numerous times, trying to identify the fifth freedom as I understood it. I told myself to be patient and wait on God and when the time was right He would reveal it to me. In analysis, discovery of the fifth freedom, Freedom from Our Enemies, is a real jewel in understanding God's word. An even greater jewel is the lesson learned, be patient and wait on the Lord to reveal the mysteries of His word. This is a major victory over Satan, the enemy, who would rather we not understand the ways of our Father.

Proverbs 16:7 says, "When a man's ways please the Lord, he maketh even his enemies to be at peace with him." This Proverb has far-reaching implications. It totally encompasses my understanding of what I have identified as the fifth freedom.

Does God Hide from Us
in Times of Trouble?

In opening this paper on the subject of "Does God Hide from Us in Times of Trouble," I would like to reflect, giving praise, honor, and thanks to our Lord and Savior Jesus Christ. When I think of his dying on the cross and what he told his Disciples in Luke 24: 49, "I am going to send you what my Father has promised, but stay in the city until you have been clothed with power from on high". It reminds me of the Holy Spirit and how essential its Being is in the life of each Christian.

"Why, O Lord, do you stand far off? Why do you hide yourself in times of trouble?" (Psalm 10:1; NIV). This one verse poses two questions. We as Christians often ask ourselves these two questions during our Christian walk and during prayer. If we don't feel God's presence in our lives daily, mostly in prayer, sickness and death of love ones, we feel abandoned. Why is this so? Jesus said to his Disciples in Matthew 8: 26 "You of little faith." Could this be the answer? As a Christian, I feel this is the answer in totality. We become accustomed to feeling God's presence and feel lonely when we can't connect with Him. Just as any parent, even in a single-child household, our Father, God, has more on His plate than just us. He is omnipresent.

I once explained, in a conversation with a stranger, the omnipresence of God in this type of situation in the following way: In times of trouble, trouble being anything that upsets the harmony of our lives, we depend on our Father to help us when called upon. We are not His only child, for all Christians are Sons and Daughters. Maybe, just maybe, one of our sisters or brothers has a problem that is more pressing than ours, and the Father sought to give them the spiritual attention they required, healing, peace of mind, or whatever is needed. This does not mean He has forgotten about us. It just means our troubles have not reached the magnitude of some of our sisters or brothers, or He has already equipped us with the required resources to solve the problem. He has promised to be with us always, in our hearts, and just because we don't feel His spiritual presence does not mean we are alone.

Psalm 46:1 reminds us that God is "an ever-present help in trouble." Although He appears not to be with us, *God is our refuge and our strength.* This is not a temporary presence. Matthew Henry writes "It is because we judge by outward appearance; we stand afar off from God by our unbelief, and then we complain that God stands afar off from us." We must learn to take God at His word, for He cannot lie.

Who, besides God's chosen, are so lucky to have Him near then whenever they pray or need help? Trust in God. Continue to pray with the Holy Spirit as your guide. The spiritual assurances you are seeking and the blessings you await will come when the time is right. They may not be everything you hoped for, but they will be what God has willed for your life. Have faith and trust because we serve an On-Time-God. Since God cannot lie, He sent us what was promised, the Holy Spirit to be our guide. We are reminded that God Does Not Hide From Us in Times of Trouble.

And the bonus is. Whenever we go through trouble or desert areas, it is a testament to our life. Anything that God allows us to endure is not just for our benefit. It is given to us as a mercy, blessing, and even as a gift to testify to others about the goodness of God in times of need. Comfort others as God has comforted you. Testify to His greatness, giving Him all the honor and praise worthy of a Father that is like none other.

Safe from Danger

As we travel through this life, we encounter situations that can place us in harm's way and open us up to physical and mental dangers. We have no way of knowing when they will appear. The one thing that is certain: they will pop up at the most unreasonable times. Christians should remember that they have a God in Heaven who is omnipresent and watches over His children at all times.

I am reminded of the Israelites plight when God resolved to bring them out of bondage. In His first set of instructions to Moses, to show him His power in Exodus Chapter 4, He used the staff in Moses' hand to prove a point. He told him to throw the staff on the ground, and it became a snake. He then told Moses to pick it up by the tail. Any snake, poisonous or not, will bite. God knew this and instructed Moses to pick the snake up by the tail. This is a very small example of God keeping us "Safe from Danger." Once we become Christians, God is always there to guard us from danger. We oftentimes call it "being lucky." God's will for our lives and protection from danger is not luck. We should learn to recognize God's hand in our lives and what He does for us in all aspects of our daily living.

In Exodus 4:17, God told Moses to take his staff in hand so he could perform miraculous signs with it. It would prove to be significant in the saving of the Israelites from Pharaoh's army. God purposely led His people on the long route to reach the Promise Land. The main reason could very well have been to show His protective powers in time of danger. The route they took led them to the Red Sea. A natural barrier was placed in front of them, and Pharaoh's army was placed behind them. To help the Israelites understand that He was their God and He would keep them "Safe from Danger," He protected their rear with a pillar of Cloud. Throughout the night, the Cloud brought darkness to one side and light to the other. Pharaoh's army could not advance because of the darkness on their side. The Israelites, on the other hand, had day light and could see the mighty hand of God at work. He told Moses to stretch out his staff over the Red Sea, and the sea parted to the left and the right. As a result, the Israelites crossed on dry land. In their attempt to pursue the Israelites, Pharaoh's army was destroyed when God released the Red Sea to its natural state. The same God in days of old is the same God today; He protects us. We are constantly being kept "Safe from Danger."

In Psalm 26, when speaking of God's integrity, David says, "For thy loving-kindness is before mine eyes." Those who do not know God cannot see what He does for them from day to day, let alone throughout their lives. But as Christians, we realize His loving kindness and are able to see His workings. We reach this point simply because we accepted Christ as our Lord and Savior and have continued to stay in constant communication with God through prayer and reading His word.

Our realization of being "Safe from Danger" is the work of God through His Holy Spirit. It is His doing, not our ability to sustain ourselves or even the luck of the draw. In Streams in the Desert, it is summed up in these words, "your weakness needs My strength, and your safety lies in letting Me fight for you." If you haven't done so, give your life to God, and if Jesus Christ is your Lord and Savior, give in to the will of God, for He will keep you "Safe from Danger."

If God Said It, He Will Perform It

"If God Said It He Will Perform It" is built around the premise that He is faithful to His word. For a better understanding of this subject, we will explore the four pillars of God's Promise. The four promises of God are found in numerous writings, and therefore the principles identified here are selected. His justice and holiness means that God would never allow Himself to deceive us; grace or goodness assures us that He will not allow Himself to forget; His word is truth and therefore it will not change; His power enables Him to accomplish all that He promises.

God created man. We are His Children, to whom He gave life by breathing His Spirit into Adam. Romans 11:33 says God's judgments are unsearchable and His ways past finding out. Isaiah 30:18 reminds us that we serve a just God. His wisdom and knowledge are so infinite that we could never understand His decisions. The justice of God is backed-up by His Holiness because He conforms to no standard. He is the standard. Since He set the standard that is above all standards and His judgments cannot be scrutinized, He cannot deceive us because He promised. Being Children of God, we are reminded in Psalm 145:13: "The Lord is faithful to all his promises and loving toward all he has made."

God's grace is unmerited favor. The good He does for us we do not deserve. His grace is sufficient and made perfect in our weakness. God loves us even when we do not know how to love ourselves. Ephesians 2:8 reminds us that God's grace is a gift. Since His grace is something He wills to His children, He is bound by His word and cannot allow Himself to forget the needs of His children.

God's word is truth and therefore it will not change. Because His word is truth, it is His sincere desire that all be saved. The promise of salvation is extended to everyone for Ephesians 1:13 reads, "And you also were included in Christ when you heard the word of truth, the gospel of your salvation". Matthew 24:14 says, "And the Gospel of the Kingdom will be preached in the whole world as a testimony to all nations, and then the end will come" and identifies when the fulfillment of the promise will be realized. This is another case in which "If God Said It He Will Perform It" because His word is truth, and until everyone has had an opportunity to be saved, the end will not come.

His power, omnipotence, enables Him to accomplish all that He promises. At the beginning of the Bible in Genesis 18:14 when God announced that Sarah would be with child, the question was asked, "Is anything too hard for God?" This simply means that God can do anything that does not contradict His nature. In the fulfillment of His power, Hebrew 2:8 states "… and put everything under His feet. In putting everything under Him, God left nothing that is not subject to Him." Jesus had walked among man, died, and was buried. God has raised Him from the dead, and He sat at the right hand of the Father. How powerful is my God? This is an even greater emphasis of "If God Said It He Will Perform It."

The Bible is God's word to the Church of Christ and the world. Just as He outlined promises and curses for the Israelites in the Old Testament, He made promises to all Christians. Familiarize yourself with those promises, and when you pray remind God of those promises. God is faithful to His word and cannot lie. Second Corinthians 1:20 reads, "For no matter how many promises God has made, they are 'Yes' in Christ." "Yes" means "Yes," and in Christ all promises are fulfilled. If this is not proof enough, why is written in the Bible. "If He Said It He Will Perform It."

God Provides

This subject, God Provides, for me has very deep emotional feelings and an urge to put those feelings in writing. Some subjects are easy to approach, and others are more difficult. Therefore, God's provision is the only thing that will allow me to deal with this subject objectively, especially knowing my love for God. I pray that the words I'm about to write will shine and offer someone new hope. "God Provides" gives new hope daily.

Where should one start? Exodus 3:14, Matthew 6:11, Luke 11:3, and Matthew 5:6 are all scriptures that come to mind when approaching or trying to find greater meaning in these words, "God Provides."

"I AM THAT I AM", Exodus 3:14, is vital to understanding this subject. First of all, it explains two of the names of God, Jehovah and Immanuel. The meaning of these two names, The One Who Is, or The Self-Existent One, and God with Us speaks volumes. We should first realize that God has His being of Himself and that He is dependent upon no one. God is thus placed in a category by Himself, above all and in all from the perspective of these two names. Being self-existent makes Him all-sufficient in that He needs nothing and all things belong to Him and all things come from Him. So through His inexhaustible resources, nothing can be lacking that is needed or wanted because "God Provides." God with Us can easily be explained by the understanding of the Holy Spirit within each Christian as it applies to us today rather than its application to the Jews of His being there whenever they needed Him. In either case, He is omnipresent.

Matthew 6:11 and Luke 11: 3, excerpts from the Lord's Prayer, read exactly the same with the exception of the words "this day" and "day by day" (KJV) or "today" and "each day" (NIV). Therefore, "Give us...our daily bread" has the same interpretation when either set of words are used. In

Old Testament terms, this can be applied to nourishment in the form of food in general or manna for the Israelites during their desert experience upon their exodus from Egypt. In the vernacular of the New Testament, we know that that our natural being is connected to our spiritual being and our daily bread supports the necessary comforts of this present life.

This verse contains several other characteristics. We ask for nourishment for our bodies. We ask for something specific, implying honesty of what nourishment is required. We ask for it today in order to meet the needs of today and not taking thought for tomorrow, for tomorrow is not promised. We ask for God's favor out of His love for us. We pray give us, showing a concern for others and their needs. And finally, in whatever form we pray daily, we ask anew, for each day's needs are different from the day before.

"God Provides" then means daily provisions. When we pray this verse or use similar words and ask in the name of Jesus Christ, we exclaim vehemently that God is our sustainer and provider. We have no misconception or notion that we can provide for ourselves. We who claim total dependence on God are assured that God will sustain and provide for us according to His omniscience of what our daily needs may be. As Christians, we are thankful and should strive every day to express this to someone in need of our Lord and Savior's saving grace.

Matthew 5:6 goes hand in hand with this verse. "Blessed are they which do not hunger and thirst after righteousness, for they shall be filled." The Liberty Bible Commentary says, "Those who are poor and empty in their own spiritual poverty recognize the depth of their need and hunger and thirst for that which only God can give them." We as Christians realize that we have a need, and that need or hunger, once we become believers, has a thirst attached to it that is a natural instinct when we are fed or eat. That inner passion, hungering and thirsting, is a Christian need that cannot be fulfilled. Therefore, our spiritual nourishment is just as important as our physical nourishment. It is a daily need.

Where does a Christian get spiritual nourishment? It comes from the Word of God. Our daily need for spiritual nourishment through staying in the Word of God implies once again that God Provides. Knowing this, we should strive vigorously to set aside time each day to pray and meditate on God's word.

Tell them that I AM sent you, I AM THAT I AM, as the answer to the question Moses asks God of how to reply if the Israelites ask who sent him is virtually the same yesterday as it is today. God is the same yesterday, today, and tomorrow. "I AM" is all that we need, physically and spiritually. God Provides.

I Will Never Leave or Forsake You

This is a very familiar subject or even saying to many of us. It is the Word of God. A statement we use to affirm our faith or allegiance to God. In time of distress or trouble, we proclaim these words to receive from God whatever it is we need in our lives. In 2 Timothy 3: 10-11 Paul tells Timothy that he knows of his sufferings and persecutions. These are only two of the areas where we never fail to call upon God for His help and mercy.

I would like to explore this subject briefly from two perspectives. One, the perspective of God's promise to us, and two, what it means as a promise from us to God that we will never leave Him or forsake Him.

Several verses in the Bible contain these words. In Deuteronomy: 31:6, 8, Moses uses the phrase "he will never leave you nor forsake you." Moses was speaking to the Israelites. He was giving them instructions on going into the Promised Land without him and under the guidance of Joshua. He reminded them of the battles they had fought against stronger opponents and how the Lord, their God, went before them in battle. This promise does not only hold true in battles but in any fight Christians find themselves in. The power of a victorious life is in God, and if we allow Him to work through us, patiently waiting on Him to do what He does best, we have the promise that He will not leave us nor forsake us.

Hebrews 13:5, 6 of the NIV says:

> *Keep your lives free from the love of money and be content with what you have, because God has said, "Never will I leave you; never will I forsake you. So we say with confidence, The Lord is my helper, I will not be afraid. What can man do to me?"*

The problem touched on here is greed. However, greed can cover a wide array of subjects and areas in our lives, such as: how much control do we want over certain situations? What am I willing to let go of in order to keep myself happy. God's stance in verse 5 is a positional stance. If we can be content in any area of our life, God has promised to be right there by our side in whatever capacity we need Him. He will be a brace to lean on, a comforter to console us, or even a stretcher to carry us. The surety in verse 6 is provisional. When we put our hopes and trust in ourselves and the things we think we have control over, there is no room left for God to work in us. However, if we put our trust in God, His presence and provisions will produce contentment. Daily we have to address areas of our lives in prayer and wait upon God to produce the desired results. Being prayed up daily provides the strength from God to endure all things that may come our way. Faith in prayer is the key. But to have faith and pray with love for God in our heart and to accept what He is willing to do in our lives according to His will is the master key. He will never leave us or forsake us.

What does it take to be content? Contentment is a state of satisfaction, or being at ease in our position in life. We have to realize God's sufficiency for our needs. We know the things we would like to have: money, a fine car, a large home and even friends on every side. These are all nice things to have. However, is this what God wants for us? In order for us to have the things our heart's desire, we first have to accept the desires of God, what He wants us to have according to our dependence upon Him for our needs. He is omnipotent, an almighty God with infinite power. He is omnipresent, everywhere at the same time including with us in all circumstances. He is omniscient, having infinite knowledge and knowing our needs and what is right for us in accordance with His will for our lives. Knowing this as Christians we can be content. How can we not understand that He will never leave us or forsake us?

Understanding God's sufficiency is to understand that He will provide all our needs. In Philippians 4:11-13, Paul writes:

> *I am not saying this because I am in need, for I have learned to be content whatever the circumstances. I know what it is to be in need, and I know what it is to have plenty. I have learned the secret of being content in any and every situation, whether well fed or hungry, whether*

living in plenty or in want. I can do everything through him who gives me strength.

Paul is saying that we have to be victorious over every circumstance and not victims of the circumstances of our lives. We can do this by simply adjusting to the will of God. Psalm 119:105 says, "Your word is a lamp to my feet and a light for my path." If we trust this saying, then we can boldly go where the finger of God points knowing that God will provide whatever we need along the way.

We could talk for days about the promise of God, "God will never leave or us or forsake us." However, what is our promise to God that we will never leave Him or forsake Him?

We can simply start with The Word as Jesus Christ and The Word as the message in the Bible. Now how does this apply to our lives?

As Christians we have declared Jesus Christ as our Lord and Savior. John tells us that "the Word was with God and the Word was God." If the Holy Trinity consists of God the Father, God the Son, and God the Holy Spirit, then we know Jesus Christ, our Lord and Savior as the second person of the Holy Trinity. John also tells us that "The Word was with God, and the Word was God." Without making this a long and drawn out subject, we simply understand, as Christians, that Jesus Christ was the Word.

In understanding the crucifixion, the Gospel of Mark 15:38 tells us that the curtain in the temple was torn in two from top to bottom at the ninth hour. Christ's crucifixion and the tearing of the curtain provided a lasting sacrifice for our sins and reopened a doorway of communication with God, the Father. Christ identifies Christians as those given to Him by His Father, and thus we have been accepted as children of God, sons and daughters of the Father. Realizing all God has done in our lives and how much He loves us, who would leave such a loving Father. Christ as the Word provided us with the opportunity of a lifetime and a loving Father we should never be able to separate ourselves from. Believing in Christ as The Word affords Christians the opportunity to say Father I will never leave you nor forsake you.

We understand that God, the Holy Spirit in us, convicts us and causes us to realize we are nothing without Him. Studying God's word gives us a greater understanding of God's will for our life. Second Timothy 2:15 states, "Do your best to present yourself to God as one approved, a workman who does not need to be ashamed and who correctly handles the word of truth." We should learn to build our lives on the Word of God. In doing so, His word will tell us how to live for Him and serve Him. When we are down and out, it is God's word that will get us through. Pray on the things that trouble you. Whether it is suffering, physically or emotionally, we should pray and remember The Word of God. By trusting His word and enduring the hardships, in God's time, the weight will lift. We will become content, filled with the Holy Spirit, because of God's love, mercy, and abiding grace for our lives.

We must learn to trust God in all things. Jesus, in speaking to his disciples in John 12:36, told them to "Put your trust in the light while you have it, so that you may become sons of light." He wanted them to understand that they should take advantage of his presence. Jesus Christ left us the Word. If we study the Word of God and walk in the in the light of Jesus Christ, we then become sons and daughters of the light. We are then, as Christians, given power to reveal the truth of the Bible and point people to God. Believing in Jesus Christ, studying God's Word, and carrying the torch lets the light of the Holy Spirit shine in and through us. We are therefore empowered to pull others into a life of joy and peace with the Father.

In closing, I would like to quote Sarah Young when she talks about trusting Jesus. She talks about how people trust and fall away. She then states,

> *Isn't it often the same way with you? You trust Me when things go well, when you see Me working on your behalf. This type of trust flows readily within you, requiring no exertion of your will. When things go wrong, your trust-flow slows down and solidifies. You are forced to choose between trusting Me intentionally or rebelling: resenting My ways with you. This choice constitutes a fork in the road. Stay on the path of Life with Me, enjoying My Presence. Choose to trust Me in all circumstances."*

If we trust in the Lord in all we do, we've solved the biggest portion of life's problems. God has provided us with everything we need, His promise, His son, and His Word. How can we leave Him or forsake Him?

Faith During Desperate Times

Sometimes we reach a point in our day or lives where everything is not progressing according to plan. We feel a need for accomplishment. Because of our humanness, we want to rush things along. We've become accustomed to making the right decisions at the right time and the right moves to meet those demands. When we reach this stage, we are short of placing ourselves in disastrous situations which could place us in a state of despair. Instead we become desperate because we are unable to accomplish or attain the desired results. These disastrous situations become Desperate Times.

C.H. Spurgeon once quoted, "God had one son without sin, but never had a son that was not tested." What does this mean in the term of Desperate Times? We know that Jesus Christ is the only Son of God that has never sinned, however, he was tested on several occasions as we are tested today. After being baptized by John the Baptist, Matthew 4:1 lets us know that "Jesus was led by the Spirit into the desert to be tempted by the devil." Three times Jesus was tempted by Satan, and three times he replied in obedience through the faith he had in his Father. These replies were Matthew 4:4, "It is written: Man does not live on bread alone, but on every word that comes from the mouth of God; Matthew 4:7, "It is also written, Do not put the Lord your God to the test"; and Matthew 4:10, "Away from me, Satan! For it is written: "'Worship the Lord Your God, and serve him only."

You may ask what temptation has to do with being tested. The answer is very simple. Temptation opens the door to compliance or obedience. That compliance or obedience then becomes a test to our will. Desperate Times are a test of our compliance or obedience to the will of God for our lives because of impatience.

Anything that puts us in opposition to God's word places us in an awkward situation. This is so because, as Christians, we know that we will not live a life free from suffering, pain, or trials. Desperate Times are a test of our faith in God. In our humanness, we cannot alleviate or sustain during any of these situations without God's help. Therefore we must humble ourselves.

During Desperate Times, our faith in a Father we have never seen but trust and believe in because of our acceptance of Jesus Christ as our Lord and Savior strengthens us. The replies Jesus gave Satan are from Deuteronomy Chapter 8. He recited these words of his Father which were given to the Israelites to remind them of what God had done for them during their desert experience and would continue to do in Canaan. Jesus was keenly aware that if they applied then, they would apply during his temptations. We can have faith today that the words given in the days of old or any scripture in the Bible apply also to our life today. Desperate Times should be recognized as building blocks of faith that lead us on a path lit by God. Desperate Times are opportunities in the school of wisdom, teaching us to live by faith and rely on God to bring us through. . Psalms 107:27-28 reads "…they were at their wits' end. Then they cried out to the Lord in their trouble, and he brought them out of their distress." God does the same for us during Desperate Times. Faith did not create these conditions, but it works to sustain us and bring us through them. All we need to do is have faith, humble ourselves, and cry out to our Father in Heaven for relief during Desperate Times.

Samaritan Example
Reveals Good Christian Values

The Bible Dictionary gives one of the descriptions of a Samaritan as a term of contempt with the Jews when spoken. This contempt or belief was because of their actions as the remnant left in the Land of Israel after the exile. They began to mingle and marry the foreigners settled in the land by the King of Assyria after his third invasion, leading to the Seventy Year exile and creating a race that was not pure. Some describe them as cousins of the Israelites. They existed as a separate people but not a nation. They were not a Godly people, but their examples in the Bible clearly exemplify that we can learn from all people.

As Christians, we have a good understanding of how we should live our lives and comply with the Word of God. Jesus used the Samaritans in several passages of the Bible to identify some good Christian values. The Parable of the Good Samaritan, Luke 10:25-37, is an excellent example.

Christian values, according to Wikipedia, historically are derived from the teachings of Jesus Christ and taught by Christians. This parable identifies Christian Values we should endeavor to achieve daily.

The Parable of the Good Samaritan in short relates to a man wounded and left beside the road for dead. Two of the people who passed him were a priest and a Levite. These two, because of their designation by God as chosen, should have rendered assistance to this man in need. Ideally, because of their chosen status, they should be teachers and doers of God's word. However, this was not the case. As it would be, a Samaritan, one despised and hated by the Jews, was the one to show true humanity toward his neighbor. This parable is the answer given in reply to a question a lawyer or man of the law asks Jesus about "what must I do to inherit eternal life?" Jesus ask him what was written in the law. He replied, "Love the Lord your God with all your heart and with all your soul and with all your mind" and "Love your neighbor as yourself." Jesus acknowledged his answer as being correct, "But he wanted to justify himself, so he asked Jesus, "Who is my neighbor.""

In this parable, we have, at a minimum, three themes at work. The main idea conveyed is in 1st Corinthians 13:13; "And these three remain: faith, hope and love. But the greatest of these is love." Love is the greatest of all Christian Values and is an attribute of God Himself. Christ taught love first, and we as Christians should do the same. John 3:16 begins, "God so loved the world that He gave His one and only son." Christ's love was so great that he died on the cross for our sins. The least we can do is love one another.

The second idea conveyed is mercy. The lawyer's hatred was so great that he could not use the word Samaritan in his reply to Jesus and simply stated, "The one who had mercy on him." Jesus, in his teaching about loving our enemies, admonishes us in Luke 6:36 to "Be merciful, just as your Father is merciful." Mercy is one of our Father's greatest perfections. If we are to imitate Jesus, who is the second in the Godhead, knowing that he does as his Father does, then we should strive to show mercy when opportunity lends itself.

The third is "Go." Charles H. Spurgeon explains it best:

> Go, and do you likewise. Here was a dismission, and here was a commission, too! Jesus dismissed him. "I have nothing more to say to you. 'Go.'" Here was the commission. "Do you likewise." Alas, I am afraid that after most sermons people get the dismission, "Go," but they forget the commission—"Go, and do you likewise." It is your privilege as well as your duty, O Christians, to assist the needy and, whenever you discover distress, as far as lies in you, to minister practically to its relief!

Therefore, our Christian values from this parable are "Love" as God would have us to do; be "Merciful" as Jesus has admonished us; and "Go" as it is the Great Commission given by Jesus Christ as a calling to his followers to take action. "Love," be "Merciful," and "Go" are three Christian Values we must employ daily.

God's Chastisement

The age-old question that gives rise to this topic is: "Why do the wicked seem to make constant progress toward reaching their goals while the righteous appear to be in constant struggles?"

One of the reasons for this is found in Proverbs 3:11-12: "My son, do not despise the Lord's discipline and do not resent his rebuke, because the Lord disciplines those He loves, as a father the son he delights in." It is not always easy to identify why things happen in our lives. These things can be stressful situations coming from combinations of events or even pain without a recognizable source. It is certain that uncomfortable situations in our lives are not always the result of God's discipline. However, there are times when God does step in, making us feel guilty, bring crisis into our lives, or even allowing us to have bad experiences because we have sinned. We look at these instances and wonder why the people doing the same things we are doing do not have the same problems we do. The answer is quite simple; God does not chastise us all in the same manner. As Christians, we acknowledge the great blessings we receive from God. It should be easy to understand that His chastening is a sign of His displeasure with our actions and His love for us because He wants us to spend eternity with Him and our Lord in Heaven.

In Hebrews 12:6, we read the same thing in a different way: "Because the Lord disciplines those He loves and punishes everyone He accepts as a son." To know that God has accepted you as a son or daughter is a blessing in itself. It is human nature not to accept discipline or punishment without some resentment. God's word in Proverbs 13:24 tell us: "He who spares the rod hates his son, but he who loves him is careful to discipline him." God knows what it takes to obtain what He has planned for our life. If He spares the rod, our steps may deviate from His word and we will not reap the reward of His love and eternal life, for Psalm 119:133 reads, "Direct my steps according to your word; let no sin rule over me". If sin is not to have dominion over us, our steps must be in accordance with the Word of God.

One of the best answers I have found to this question is Psalm 11:5: "The Lord examines the righteous, but the wicked and those who love violence his soul hates." The Life Application Study Bible's explanation to this verse is:

> *God does not shield believers from difficult circumstances but he tests both the righteous and the wicked. For some, God's tests become a refining fire, while for others; they become an incinerator for destruction. Do not ignore or defy the test and challenges that come your way. Use them as opportunities for you to grow.*

The wicked will receive theirs in due time. That is not for Christians to worry about because Christ will judge all. Be comfortable in your present situation, trust in the Lord, and wait patiently for Him to work out His plan for your life. To obtain peace, we must learn from our trials and yield to God's word, giving Him complete control of our lives. God's Chastisement results in the desires of our hearts. A better life, less stress and a place in Glory.

Molding Our Personality

Let's set the stage for this subject. Psalm 101 and the Holy Spirit blessed my soul this morning. The author in one of my commentaries described Psalm 101 as penmanship by David, saying, "The subject of the psalm is rightful conduct and proper principles for the rule of a godly king." Charles H. Spurgeon wrote, "After songs of praise a psalm of practice not only makes variety, but comes in most fittingly. We never praise the Lord better than when we do those things which are pleasing in his sight." Then the Life Application Study Bible identifies it as: "A prayer for help to walk a blameless path. To live with integrity, both our efforts and God's help are necessary."

The life we live takes shape as we walk the path. The path can be a path with or without Christ. I've come to understand that a path filled with the Holy Spirit leading me daily through the Word of God is the only way. Some began this journey earlier than others and are on the path longer. Matthew Henry wrote, "Many who begin last, and promise little in religion, sometimes, by the blessing of God, arrive at greater attainments in knowledge, grace, and usefulness, than others whose entrance was more earlier, and who promised fairer." However, the quantification of the change does not matter. The point of it all is who we are changes and so does our personality as we spend time in God's Word and grow to be more like Jesus. Psalm 101 outlines several things David wanted to master, which can be helpful to us in our walk with God. Two things that really stand out for me in this Psalm, as written in the KJV, are "A forward heart shall depart from me" and "I will early destroy all the wicked of the land."

Thomas Chalmers understands forwardness as "from-wardness" and says, in the Liberty Commentary, that it is "giving way to sudden impulses of anger, or quick conception, and casting it forth in words or deeds of impetuous violence." Therefore, "a forward heart shall depart from me" means that I will change those things, be they my surroundings or personal attributes, which cause me to make certain rash decisions using God's Word as my standard-bearer. The Holy Spirit, through God's Word, will enable me to do good when I would have otherwise done wrong. Second Timothy 2:15-17 (NIV), "Do your best to present yourself to God as one approved, a workman who does not need to be ashamed and who correctly handles the word of truth." Growth in this aspect of life is a real game changer and molds our personality to conform to the will of God.

"I will early destroy all the wicked of the land." David made a conscious decision that each morning he would root out the wicked. Day after day, he would continue to do this. If we take on this persona, praying to God for strength daily, the person we used to be, according to the will of God, will change, making us more Christlike.

The Parable of the Hidden Treasure, Matthew 13:44, helps us to realize that once we've begun on the path, one that leads to eternal life, we must be willing to give up those worldly valuables or values that hinder our walk. Andrew Murray, in God's Best Secrets, "Christ claims the whole heart, the whole life, and the whole strength if we are indeed to share with Him in His victory through the power of the Holy Spirit."

Paul says, "I consider everything a loss compared to the surpassing greatness of knowing Christ Jesus." The path we chose to walk as Christians is one well worth it. Molding our Personality is changing those things about us and our lives that are contrary to God's word. It's not easy. The struggle is daily, not sometimes. As lovers of our most precious Lord and Savior Jesus the Christ, and with the help of the great I AM, "we can do this."

The Lamb

One would think that as Christians we all understand the word "lamb" when it comes to the Bible. This is not always the case. Many of us go to Church every week, hear this word, and think nothing of it. This is also the case with a significant amount of God's word that we hear and read. The problem comes when we do not take the time to find out what the meaning is and understand God's word better. Let's make it a practice to ask questions in the right environment, Sunday school, Bible Study, or other religious settings that offer an opportunity to learn when we are unsure and do not understand something about God's Word.

The relationship of the lamb in the Old and New Testament have physical as well as spiritual meanings. In the Old Testament, we are aware of the ten plagues God sent upon Egypt. We realize their significance as being designed to force Pharaoh to let the Israelites leave Egypt. After Pharaoh agrees to let the Israelites go under limited conditions, God hardens his heart because He knows that the necessary change in Pharaoh's heart was not at the point of complete submission to His will. We will never be able to understand God's ways, but we can trust that they are for our good and never to harm His chosen children, the Israelites then and all mankind now. The Plague of the Firstborn was the tenth and final plague. It achieved total submission by Pharaoh to let the Israelites go and a willingness by the Egyptian people as a whole to help them on their journey.

It is out of this tenth plague we discover The Lord's Passover and the Passover Lamb. Exodus 12 gives the whole story. One note of interest is that The Passover Lamb could be taken from the flock of the sheep or goat and had to meet the physical requirements, preparation, and consumption requirements specified to Moses by God. This can be confirmed in Exodus 12:3-6. The Bible Dictionary tells us that "lamb" is a translation of several

Hebrew words in the English Bible, with most of them referring to the young of the sheep. However, the Hebrew meaning for the word sheh is used in Exodus 12:3-6 and refers to the young of either sheep or goats and seems to include adult specimens at times. The Passover Lamb was to be slaughtered at twilight on the fourteenth day of the month. Some of the blood was to be put on the sides and tops of the doorframes of the houses where they ate the lamb, meaning the homes of the Israelites. The resulting significance, as written in the NIV, is:

> *On that night I will pass through Egypt and strike down every firstborn – both men and animals – and I will bring judgment on all the gods of Egypt. I am the Lord. The blood will be as a sign for you on the houses where you are; and when I see the blood, I will pass over you. No destructive plague will touch you when I strike Egypt.*

Hence we have The Lord's Passover and the Passover Lamb.

In the New Testament, the Apostle John introduces us to the Lamb of God. Jesus was called the Lamb of God by John the Baptist in John 1:29 and 36, "Look, the Lamb of God." The significance of this phrase would become central to the point of Jesus being crucified or led off to be slaughtered as a lamb. Isaiah 53:7, "He was oppressed and afflicted, yet he did not open his mouth, he was led like a lamb to be slaughtered," and again in Acts 8:32 when Philip asks the eunuch what he is reading and then explains to him the good news of Jesus. In Revelations 5:6-16, John speaks of seeing a lamb looking as if it had been slain, in reference to Jesus.

There are other distinctions between the Passover Lamb and Jesus that we can see in scripture. For instance, it was to be without defect, and 1Peter 1:19 reads, "a lamb without blemish or defect, denoting the purity of Jesus." The lamb was chosen on the tenth of the month and slaughtered on the fourteenth of the month, four days later. Jesus was crucified on the Passover and had entered Jerusalem four days prior. Even in the regulations for the continued observance of the Passover, Exodus 12:46 says, "Do not break any bones." This same passage is attributed to the crucifixion in John 19:36: "Not one of his bones will be broken."

Physical application in the Old Testament is described by its blood being used in the identification of homes in the deliverance of the Israelites from the oppression of slavery under Egyptian rule and as a sacrifice. It is spiritual because God, Yahweh, accomplished the action. The remembrance of what God had done for them had a spiritual connection as described in the establishment and observance of the Lord's Passover. Exodus 12:42 explains it this way. "Because the Lord kept vigil that night to bring them out of Egypt, on this night all the Israelites are to keep vigil to honor the Lord for the generations to come." A special connection with God to remind them who He is and where He brought them from. Also a reminder that He is willing to meet their needs for He hears their cry for help, as seen over and over again in scripture. The Lamb is physical in the New Testament in Jesus being led off to Golgotha to be slaughtered. Spiritually, we cannot deny the incarnation of God in human form. Additionally, in John's vision in Revelations, the lamb is depicted as one looking as if it had been slain and standing in the center of the throne. His bloody body symbolizes His submission to God's will and the purchase of men for God. Just as the blood of a lamb was used to deliver the Israelites from slavery under Egyptian rule, man was delivered from the slavery of sin, introduced into the world with the disobedience of Adam and Eve, by the blood of Jesus.

I find understanding of Bible scripture intelligently stimulating when looking at the depth of the Old Testament's relationship to the New Testament. The more we study and understand, the more God can reveal to us. The foretelling of the coming of The Messiah in the Old Testament has eternal significance, but the information on knowing the physical and spiritual role played by the lamb as a symbol with two different associations is too powerful to neglect. Simply stated, we had to have Jesus before He could be sacrificed as a Lamb.

Lord Jesus Christ

We often hear the term "Lord Jesus Christ!" Matthew Henry describes this as three names of one person, denoting the threefold office of God the Son. Lord as a universal king, Jesus as a Priest, and Christ as a Prophet. Each of these three offices will be discussed separately in an effort to enhance the understanding of those of us who have not viewed the Lord Jesus Christ as a person with varying roles. Jesus Christ in his authority as the Son of God holds a threefold office in his relationship to human kind, as the Holy Trinity holds a relationship to our Salvation.

The Holy Trinity consisting of God the Father, God the Son, and God the Holy Spirit are one. This we know as Christians. It may have taken some of us a little time to grasp the concept, but we finally got it. For me, after I got it, later in life, God took it a little farther. The distance to which He has taken me boils down to: what do I really know about the Holy Trinity? I prayed to God for a better understanding and found that it is far more than I imagined. The working of the Holy Trinity is where the Spirit led me. My study and knowledge allowed me to focus on God the Son, Jesus. I'm beginning to learn, each day, just how important He is in our lives.

C. C. Ryrie writes, "There is only one God, but in the unity of the Godhead there are three external and coequal Persons, the same in substance, but distinct in subsistence." It is in the distinct subsistence where the answer lies. Subsistence philosophically means "of an independent entity; the quality of having a timeless or abstract existence; mode of existence or that by which a substance is individualized." Does this in some way describe the Alpha and Omega of God with individuality as three in one?

In our quest to know more about Jesus, we must read the Bible with a passion sparked and led by the guidance of the Holy Spirit. It will help us to understand His role as Prophet, Priest, and King. Just as C. C. Ryrie explained, the Godhead as the same in substance but distinct in subsistence we are now able to see Jesus in a different light. The threefold office of Lord Jesus Christ allows Him to take us on a path of learning through the word; a path of understand through His sacrifice and a Priest of the most high God; and then see Him in His position of King as the Father placed all things under His feet; and as a prophet, for he often referred to his words being those of the Father.

The Old Testament foretold these things long before the coming of Christ. The New Testament in a sense allows the predictions to unfold or serves as confirmation of them. Lord Jesus Christ is Prophet, Priest, and King of the children of God.

Lord, Lord, Lord

"Lord, Lord, Lord" is a conscious effort to explain Jesus in His office of universal king, as part of the title Lord Jesus Christ where Jesus is King, Priest, and Prophet. In the Old Testament, we see "Lord" used in two different contexts. "Lord" makes reference to the Lord Almighty in lieu of God in the Old Testament, and "Lord" is also used to describe earthly kings. In the New Testament, we have Lord Jesus Christ and the Lord God Almighty. It is used is in relation to Jesus Christ and the Father. "Lord" can be defined in terms of how it relates to man and his positions and then as in reverence, according to the Webster Dictionary, as The Supreme Being, Jehovah and The Savior, Jesus Christ.

Jews gave great reverence to God, and out of that great reverence, whenever they had a need to read or say the name God, they replaced it with Adonai which means Lord. Instead of Lord God Almighty as we say it today, they would use the term Lord Almighty. The meaning and importance of who God is did not change. Psalm 144:15 exemplifies this by saying "blessed are the people whose God is the Lord". There can be no substitution of the fact that God is creator and sustainer of all and our prosperity depends on His faithfulness to His Word.

Kings in the Old Testament were often referred to as "Lord" since the word applied to both God and man, expressing different degrees of honor, dignity, and majesty. In 1 Samuel 8, we read how the period of the Judges came to an end. Samuel, in his golden years, appointed his sons Joel and Abijah to be judges over Israel. However, they did not walk in his ways, so the elders of Israel gathered and came to Samuel. They had come to the conclusion that they wanted a King to lead them like all the other nations. As a result of the aforementioned conclusions, God granted their wish and the Israelites received their first king in the anointing of Saul.

Jesus as King and Lord is supported in Scripture. Jeremiah 23:5 talks about raising up a righteous Branch in David's place, a King who will reign wisely. In John 12:14, it is stated that "Jesus found a young donkey and sat upon it, as it is written," referring to the words of Zechariah 9:9 as the king of Israel coming. Psalm 110:1, "The Lord says to my Lord: "Sit at my right hand until I make your enemies a footstool for your feet." This confirms that David in the Psalms considered the Messiah to be his Lord who sits at the right hand of the Father, who is also Lord. Jesus confirms that he is a king when Pilate asks him if he was the King of the Jews and he replies, "Yes, it is as you say." Additionally, a king would not refer to himself as a king unless he has a kingdom. Jesus, in John 18:36, again in replying to Pilate, says, "My kingdom is not of this world," and in 37, "you are right in saying I am a king." I don't know how often Scripture identifies Jesus as a king, but I do know that God is a God that cannot lie as referenced in Numbers 23:19; 1 Samuel 15:29; Titus 1:2 and Hebrews 6:18. If it is in the Word of God, The Bible, it cannot be denied.

Revelations 1:8 reads, "I am the Alpha and the Omega," says the Lord God, "'who is, and who was, and who is to come, the Almighty." Spurgeon, in his Commentary on Great Chapters of the Bible compiled by Tom Carter, writes:

> *These are the words of the Father yet later in the book the Lord Jesus also calls himself "the Alpha and the Omega" (Rev 21:6; 22:13). We cannot always draw the line between the voice of God and the voice of the God-man, Christ Jesus, nor do we wish to do so. Yet it is always true that Christ is truly God and Scripture can speak of him either as the absolute God or as the God-man.*

If God is Lord Almighty and Lord God Almighty and Jesus is Alpha and Omega and we believe in the Holy Trinity, then "Lord" in reference to Jesus as Universal King is true as confirmed by the Lord's Word.

Jesus as Priest

The Lord Jesus in the office of Priest is one of the threefold offices identified by Matthew Henry. It may be of interest to note that Calvin and Wesley have both discussed the threefold office of Jesus in their writings. One of the functions of Jesus the Priest is Mediator. It is not a new teaching and one which we deal with quite often. In most cases we refer to a mediator as an intermediary between parties. However, there is one aspect that I never really considered. The process is a two-way street, hence the phrase "when prayers go up, blessings come down."

First and foremost, we must be aware of the workings of the Holy Trinity. He is in operation in everything, and remember that God is in control.

In Psalm 99:6, it proclaims, "Moses and Aaron were among the priests." We know and understand that the priests were the go-betweens for man and God during Old Testament times. Under the New Covenant, Jesus became Priest forever under the order of Melchizedek, Hebrews 7. Jesus' death and resurrection bridged the gap between man and God that had been severed when Adam fell from Grace. Jesus, who sits at the right hand of the Father, became our go between and once again allowed us access to a God of Grace.

All Christians realize that when we pray through the Holy Spirit in the name of Jesus, He relays our prayer to God the Father. We realize that prayer is guided by the Holy Spirit and when we cannot find the right words the Holy Spirit helps us as explained in Romans 8:26-27 (NIV):

> *In the same way, the Spirit helps us in our weakness. We do not know what we ought to pray for, but the Spirit himself intercedes for us with groans that words cannot*

express. And he who searches our hearts knows the mind of the Spirit, because the Spirit intercedes for the saints in accordance with God's will.

Once again, we should realize that the Godhead is at work. This process is one part of that two-way street; prayers go up. We should also realize that for a prayer to be answered, it must first meet the requirement of being in line with the will of God and Jesus for our life. Therefore the blessing we receive or the answer to our prayer is the will of God.

What really amazed me is blessings come down. We as humans take so much for granted. We automatically conclude that all things come from God, which is true, but we forget about Jesus' role in the process as Priest and even greater the role of the Holy Spirit. 1 Corinthians 8:6 (NIV) says, "Yet for us there is but one God, the Father from whom all things come...; and there is but one Lord, Jesus Christ, through whom all things come." Blessings come down simply means that blessings come from God through Jesus Christ to us for understanding by way of the Holy Spirit, for without God's Holy Spirit we would not be able to discern what comes from the Father through the Son.

How thankful I am for Jesus. Just knowing how He works in the life of Christians is astonishing. Where would we be without Him and His sacrifice? Every day as we pray, we should thank God for Jesus, our Priest.

Jesus as the Priest of the most High God served with distinction while walking among man. He spoke God's word to man, sacrificed himself on the Cross, was raised from the dead to sit at the right hand of the Father to receive our prayers and then dispatch a reply that we may know and be witnesses to God's blessings.

Christ the Prophet

There is no doubt that God is in control. This subject is undisputable. He is in operation in everything. I also find that when it comes to Christians, the Holy Trinity is in operation in everything also. By His incarnation, He, Jesus, took on human form to reveal God more fully and to redeem man. We find that he gave up a portion of His deity to walk among man on earth and satisfy the requirement of redeeming man to God. We have concluded that Christ is a Prophet by office per Matthew Henry and we can readily see this in the life of Jesus.

What is a prophet? Wikipedia describes a prophet in religious terms as "an individual who is claimed to have been contacted by the supernatural or the divine, and to speak for them, serving as an intermediary for humanity, delivering the new found knowledge from the supernatural entity to other people." This is basically the same meaning we give to prophets in the Bible, exclaiming that they are spokesmen for God through the operation of the Holy Spirit. He, the Holy Spirit, is distinct in subsistence also. John 14:18, "I will not leave you as orphans, I will come to you." This is Jesus' promise of the Holy Spirit to take His place and reside in His disciples and referring to Himself as the Holy Spirit. Some of the functions of the Holy Spirit are to bring to remembrance, intercede, and inspire Scripture by speaking through prophets.

There are numerous Scripture where Jesus defers His teaching and words of saving grace to God the Father. Peter reminds us in 2 Peter 1 that "no prophecy of Scripture came about by the prophet's own interpretation." Additionally, he said, "For prophecy never had its origin in the will of man" reminding us that everything originates with God. John 7: 16 says, "My teaching is not my own. It comes from him who sent me," referring to his Father in Heaven. John 12: 49-50 says, "For I speak not of my own accord, but the Father who sent me commanded me what to say and how to say it. I know his command leads to eternal life. So whatever I say is just what the Father has told me to say." Jesus in John 14: 24 says, "These words you here are not my own, they belong to the Father who sent me."

We realize that the only way to interpret a message from God is through the Holy Spirit, and Jesus has already said that He speaks the words of His Father. Putting this all together, along with the role of a prophet, we have the Holy Trinity at work. We have God the Father sending a message through God the Holy Spirit to Jesus, God the Son to be passed on to humanity for deliverance, guidance and redemption. In the receipt and deliverance of these messages we have Christ, The Prophet, not like a prophet of old but as God the Son and Prophet because he was God in human form.

Matthew 13: 57, "And they were offended in him. But Jesus said unto them, A prophet is not without honor, save in his own country." John 4:44 and Luke 7:23 are additional scripture with the same message. Believe the word.

Father, I Have No Son

I know this subject may sound dim, but the impact it has on some Christians is enormous. How do I know this? I am one of those who have no son. Sons played an important role in Old Testament times and play just as big a role now. Over the years, many questions of old have become the questions of now. I have no one to carry own my name, especially if you're the last surviving male in the family tree and you have no son. Sons today are important to mothers also, but they may see them in a different light than a father.

Why am I even discussing this subject? I pondered over this dilemma. Then one day, while studying my Bible readings for that day, I ran across a passage in the Bible that made me feel a lot better. I have a daughter, and the passage I read gave me great joy and enlightenment. That particular passage or scripture is Psalm 127:3. The NIV version reads, "Sons are a heritage from the Lord, children a reward from him." This lifted my heart and helped me to realize how blessed I was. It became one of those scriptures that I wanted to remember and refer to from time to time. I highlighted it in my Matthew Henry Commentary but did not mark the page. For quite a while, I've been looking for that scripture. Then I quit looking, reminding myself that God would reveal it to me again when the time was right. I finally ran across it again while studying the Psalms. I will never lose that page again, for the comforting words are something I need from time to time. This may even turn out to be the same for someone else.

Matthew Henry, in explaining this passage using the KJV version of the scripture, says it this way:

> *Children are God's gift and they are to us what he makes them, comforts or crosses. Children are a heritage, and a reward, and are so to be accounted, blessings and burdens;*

for he that sends mouths will send meat if we trust in him.
Children are a heritage for the Lord, as well as from him.
The family that has a large stock of children is like a quiver
full of arrows, of different sizes we may suppose, but all of
use one time or other; children of different capabilities and
inclinations.

In addition to Matthew Henry, the Liberty Commentary adds another twist:

Children are a heritage that Jehovah must give. Given this
biblical perspective on children, it is little wonder that the
people of God always abhor abortion. "The fruit of the
womb is his reward. God gives children, not as a penalty,
but as a privilege."

There is much food for thought in these two explanations of this passage of scripture, and I realize that they open up a slew of questions, but let's not lose focus. I am blessed. First off God gave me a gift, a daughter. Anytime we receive something from God, we should cherish that something with all our heart and soul. The gift of life is precious. You may not have a son to carry on your name, but a daughter is a reward of great multitude with just as many blessings, even if she does not bear children. Be thankful. God hid this scripture and interpretation from me for quite some time until I really needed it again. I thank Him for not forgetting about me. Father, I love you, even though I have no son.

Life is Precious

Life is precious. We read in Genesis that God spoke all things into being. However, Genesis 2:7 says, "the Lord God formed the man from the dust of the ground and breathed into his nostrils the breath of life, and the man became a living being." God considered man special and therefore took special care to give him a part of Himself, His breath of life. Life is a gift from God, to be valued and protected. This protection can come in one of two ways, physical or spiritual. To spiritually take care of the life God has given us, we need His word to show us the way. In reading, studying, and living His word, we make decisions that affect our lives and the lives of others.

Before I began to really study and read God's word, I had no opinion on abortion. It was fine with me, and it was the decision of those involved. I did not see this as a spiritual issue but only a moral one. Through time, I've come to see things different. God has a way of making us see things His way if we just trust Him and continue in His word. I am blessed because just as He helped me to understand this issue, He continues daily to help navigate this worldly journey as I ask Him daily to give me what He has promised, daily bread if I just ask for it.

Before I was even convinced on how I really felt about this issue, I can recall a conversation where someone asked me when life began. My answer to them, before I even had a chance to think, was at conception. I did not come to this conclusion of myself, but through the Holy Spirit, which over time has been shaping me into what God has planned for my life.

As time continues, my study of Bible scripture began to explain this subject even clearer. So much of what we say, do, and write are intertwined, and we never realize it until the Holy Spirit points it out to us. Before writing on this subject, I wrote "Father, I Have No Son." It has only been about a week now.

But that writing opened the door for God to reveal something else just as important. "Life Is Precious" and sealed my thoughts on abortion.

The Liberty Commentary gives a partial explanation of Psalm 127-3 as "Children are a heritage that Jehovah must give. Given this biblical perspective on children, it is little wonder that the people of God always abhor abortion." As explained and discussed earlier, I really had no opinion one way or the other on the matter of abortion. But this set my mind into motion, and God knew He had to work it out as part of my salvation.

To seal the deal, while reading Psalm 139, specifically verses 13-16, the interpretation from several of my commentaries gave me a clear understanding on the subject and erased all doubt. The guiding of the Holy Spirit helped me to understand that life really does begin at conception. Something I had attested to months earlier but did not have a full understanding of was now being confirmed.

Even Job was aware of the fact that his life was a gift from God and speaks thus, "clothe me with skin and flesh and knit me together with bones and sinews" (10:11)." I liken this to be close to saying what verse Psalm 139:13 says, "For you created my inmost being; you knit me together in my mother's womb" (NIV). God made us in secret, and no man is able to explain the way He does things. Spurgeon writes, "A great artist will often labour alone in his studio, and not suffer his work to be seen until it is finished; even so did the Lord fashion us when no eye beheld us, and the veil was not lifted till every member was complete."

This is not a point of contention for me. Simply stated, my study of God's word and my love for Him and His way enabled me to arrive at a personal conviction on the subject of abortion. It is my joy that some may read this and come to the same conclusion if they have had trouble understanding it or have not formed an opinion on the subject. "Life Is Precious" and "Thou shalt not kill" were given to us because we should cherish what God gives us and Praise Him for His gift of life. Matthew Henry says, "I will praise thee, the author of my being; my parents were only instruments of it."

Foreigner in Christ

Who is a foreigner? Several meanings are given to this word. A couple of those are "a person not native to or naturalized in a given country or a person born in, belonging to, or characteristic of some place or country other than the one under consideration." "Foreigner in Christ" utilizes this view as its central theme.

As a former military person, I was privileged to be stationed in Germany on several occasions. I realized the fact that I was from another country and would not be considered as a member of that country. The only way I could become a member of that country would be to denounce my American citizenship. My physical makeup distinguished me as a foreigner. However, laying that aside, the language was the most significant barrier. If I had taken the time to study and learn the language, then my acceptance would have been even greater because of the effort I put forth to understand the language and the people. I did not spend that time, and therefore was limited in my communication skills and in all areas of life which brought me into contact with the customs that were generic to that country.

Paul touches on this subject in 1 Corinthians 14:10-11. "Undoubtedly there are all sorts of languages in the world, yet none of them is without meaning. If then I do not grasp the meaning of what someone is saying, I am a foreigner to the speaker and he is a foreigner to me." Paul is talking about speaking in tongues. A Foreigner in Christ for me has a kingdom and language element.

From a kingdom perspective, Jesus told Nicodemus that a man cannot enter the kingdom of God unless he is born again. Jesus is here talking about a renewing of self. This is a change internally from that of the flesh into that of the Spirit. This inward change can only be accomplished in one way.

Matthew 10:32 of the NIV says, "Whoever acknowledges me before men, I will also acknowledge him before my Father in heaven." 1 John 4:15 says, "If anyone acknowledges that Jesus is the son of God, God lives in him and he in God." And then we have that all familiar verse, John 14:6, "I am the way the truth and the life. No one comes to the Father except through me." It is here, in these verses, clearly stated that to enter into the kingdom of God, one must first accept Jesus Christ as the Son of God and as his Lord and Savior. This acceptance does not remove you from that list of those who are Foreigners in Christ, but it is the most vital step in the process.

This kingdom perspective is also addressed by William Law when he writes on the Spirit of God and The Kingdom of Heaven. In speaking on Matthew 6:10, "your kingdom come, your will be done, on earth as it is in heaven," he writes:

> God's kingdom in heaven is the manifestation of what God is and what He does in His heavenly creatures. His will is done there because His Holy Spirit is the life, the power and the mover of everything that lives in heaven....God's kingdom comes where every other power besides His is at an end and has been driven out. His will can only be done where the Spirit that wills in God also wills in the creature.

Law speaks of God's kingdom in heaven but also of the fact that we must change or rid ourselves of all outside forces that keep us from accepting Christ as our Lord and Savior. God's Holy Spirit is manifested in us when we reach that point.

The next step is the language barrier. Proverbs 12:8 says, "A man is praised according to his wisdom." God's word is his language. The understanding of God's word leads to wisdom and each man will we rewarded accordingly. Our initial wisdom or understanding of the language of God is exemplified in Mark 10:15 in showing that anyone who does not enter and receive the kingdom of God like a child cannot enter it. We are like a child growing in stages. The same is true in understanding of God's word. Daily reading, meditation, and praying for understanding is a must. God's word is living word, and as we grow we understand more. Isaiah 55:9 helps us to realize that God's thoughts are higher than our thoughts, and our understanding of His word is according to His will for us. That understanding may lead some of us to teach or even preach God's words but that is to be determined by the will of God. The main thing to remember is that we must stay in the Word in order to understand God and His will for our lives. We will never know it all, but it is a lifelong and life sustaining journey once we have made the first step.

Putting these things together, we can come to a clear picture of what I call a Foreigner in Christ. We live in a worldly kingdom and God's kingdom is spiritual. God reigns in us though His Spirit, but He also reigns in His heavenly kingdom. To enter into that heavenly kingdom, we must first accept Jesus Christ as our Lord and Savior. Once we've done this, we must strive daily to understand the language of God, His Word. Foreigners in Christ means that the only way to transition from this state, worldly, to the next, spiritual, is to be called home to Glory. Christ is in God's heavenly kingdom with the Father in glory. The kingdom he left to reconcile man back to God. We are no longer foreigners when we join Christ in God's heavenly kingdom which is spiritual. We become citizens of God's kingdom and no longer Foreigners in Christ.

Good Friday was a Must

God's plan in the creation was to have a place where He could commune with man. A place that was perfect in all its existence. To accomplish this, God planted a garden in the east, in Eden; and there he put the man. In this garden, as we all know, were the tree of life and the tree of the knowledge of good and evil. Adam was given explicit instructions that he could eat from any tree in the garden but that he must not eat from the tree of the knowledge of good and evil.

The Bible also tells us that Adam was put in the garden to take care of it. Genesis 2:18 tells us that "The Lord God said, "'It is not good for the man to be alone. I will make a helper suitable for him." However, God had given Adam instructions prior to Eve's coming on the scene. It can be concluded that Adam explained God's instructions to Eve because she told Satan that God said, "You must not eat from the tree in the middle of the garden, and you must not touch it, or you will die." Eve, who had free reign of the garden, found herself separated from Adam near the tree of the knowledge of good and evil. This was an opportune time for Satan to tempt her, since she was separated from Adam and it is easier to conquer one than is it to conquer two united in God. She was deceived and ate of the tree of the knowledge of good and evil. However, on the other hand, Adam had been instructed by God not to eat of this tree. He allowed Eve's weakness to influence him. If he had not eaten of the tree of the knowledge of good and evil, nothing would have changed, since God had given him the instruction to refrain from this temptation. Because of his disobedience, he ate from the tree of the knowledge **of** good and evil and sin entered into the world. Adam's disobedience placed a barrier between God and man.

God, being who He is, omnipresent, omnipotent and omniscient, knew in advance that this would happen and had already devised a plan for its correction. Numerous commentaries and other books relating to biblical study see Genesis 3:15 as the evidence that Satan would be defeated and salvation would be offered to the world. The Bible, from the books of Genesis to Revelation, slowly unveils God's plan.

In the formulation and execution of God's plan, we have Exodus and the plight of the Israelites. They were chosen to further God's plan of reconciliation with man. He instructed them to build a tabernacle, which symbolized many things. One of the most important features is the curtain that separated the Holy Place from the Most Holy Place and the fact that the people could not go before God to atone for their sins. Their failure to follow the Laws of God given to Moses and failure to comply with the described blessings of God given through Moses resulted in their exile and departure from the protection of God. However, He kept His promise for them to return to their Homeland after seventy years, and they once again began to worship the God of their fathers. However, from Malachi to Matthew, not one single divine person appears, resulting in four hundred years of silence or no divine word from God.

In the Old Testament, this plan was revealed through several people in several books with scriptures that are messianic in nature. We have those in the Psalms such as 2:1-12; 16:7-11, 22; 110-1; and 118:22. We also see scriptures that are messianic in nature in books such as Isaiah, Jeremiah, Daniel, Micah and Zechariah. Specifically, Isaiah 7:14, "Therefore the Lord himself will give you a son. The virgin will be with child and will give birth to a son, and will call him Immanuel." Then we have Isaiah 9:6-7, "For to us a child is born, to us a son is given, and the government will be on his shoulders. And he will be called Wonderful Counselor, Mighty God, Everlasting Father; Prince of Peace…The zeal of the Lord Almighty will accomplish this."

Knowing that God always keeps His word, the foregoing struggles of the Israelites, prophecies and predictions came to pass. A savior was born, Jesus Christ. The Gospels explain his life from four different perspectives, giving us a clear understanding of who Jesus was. These views all add up to the conclusion that "Good Friday was a Must.". Jesus accepted responsibility for what Adam had done through his disobedience and gave himself as a sacrifice. As a result of Christ's death on the cross, we have his resurrection as proof of life after death along with the receiving of the Holy Spirit. Good

Friday was a Must; Christ's death resulted in the tearing of the curtain in the tabernacle which separated the Holy Place from the Most Holy Place, reconciling man to God again. A risen Jesus Christ gave us the assurance that God's word is truth and the Holy Spirit which allows us to understand God's will for our lives with the expressed purpose of eternal happiness in heaven. Good Friday, the crucifixion of Jesus Christ, really was a must. God knew it from the beginning.

Tithing

Sometimes we have problems understanding issues that arise in the Church and seek therefore guidance. In most cases we go to our pastor or someone of the faith who is an elder and ask for guidance or understanding. However, there are times when an answer from God is the only way to satisfy your own personal and spiritual need for understanding. This is a subject that troubled me. It troubled me because of the things I see take place. We can never know the circumstances surrounding all situations and can only pray that God helps us to understand and accept. If it is God's will, we may someday know the full truth surrounding any particular situation in mind.

We all know what tithes are. The problem comes in with the Old Testament meaning and the non-inclusion of the word tithe being specifically addressed in the New Testament as ten percent after the death of Jesus. Jesus spoke of tithes to the Pharisees because he was still in the world and the old covenant was still in effect. However, he tried to get them to see the changes that were coming into the world because of his mission from God. Several of the things they were currently doing would have to be continued in order to meet the needs of God's people and the Church. There are many truths in the Old Testament that are relevant in our lives today. I believe tithing is one of those issues.

Old Testament tithes can be easily explained. Leviticus 27:30-33 sums it up to mean everything from the land, whether grain from the soil or fruit from the trees; the entire tithe of the heard and flock – every tenth animal that passes under the shepherd's rod. These belong to the Lord and are Holy to the Lord. In the New Testament, it has been explained as the motive for giving as outlined in 2 Corinthians 9:7 as "Each man should give what he has decided in his heart to give, not reluctantly or under compulsion, for God loves a cheerful giver." The preceding verse tells us that God responds to a cheerful giver according to how they sow. Every person has a right to attend church because that is the will of God. Tithing comes with trusting the Lord to meet our needs. If over time we stop sowing or never meet the call, there is a problem in our life that only God can solve. To stop sowing is not the will of God, for God wants to bless us abundantly. Whether a person gives or not is not for me to be concerned about. I should pray for them and ask God to fix whatever it is that causes them not to give or to stop giving. There are some spiritual requirements we are mandated to meet. We have wants we can forgo to give what belongs to God because he has promised to meet all our needs.

We must remember that Jesus came to fulfill the law, not to replace it, and make it easier to live under the requirement of a Holy God. Therefore, I believe that even though the New Testament does not specifically identify giving ten percent after the death of Jesus it does say that we are to support the needs of the Church. Paul spoke several times on the principle of giving to help the Church and the poor. The proper administration of the Church of our Lord and Savior Jesus Christ is the obligation of every Christian. Giving back ten percent of what God has given you is a small price to pay, for everything belongs to God.

Additionally, the Bible tells us that a servant is worthy of his hire. The idea here, as explained in the Liberty Commentary, is "that the preacher of the gospel is to be supported by the free-will contributions of those to whom he ministers." Tithing allows Christians to meet this requirement along with the other spiritual and material needs of the Church. We are only giving back a portion of what God has allowed us to be stewards over. In giving this small amount, we will never be able to repay God for all He does and has blessed us with.

Since so many realize that the New Testament does not specifically say tithe in relation to support of the church, it does refer to the giving: For instance Matthew 6:1-4 on giving to the poor; as mentioned before, Matthew 10:10 on a servant being worthy of his hire; 1 Corinthians 16:2, "On the first day of every week, each of you should set aside a sum of money in keeping with his income, saving it up, so that when I come no collection will have to be made."; 2 Corinth 8:2-5 when Paul encourages generosity; and once again 2 Corinthians 9:6-7 on sowing and reaping. If you have a problem with tithing or its not being specifically referenced in the New

Testament as part of the new covenant, GIVE so that the storehouse may be full enough to meet the needs of the Church.

Be honest with yourself about what you are willing to do for God, for he knows your heart. Personally, I believe something is better than nothing, and I also believe ten percent is a starting point. Then, as God continues to bless you and your income increases, giving should increase proportionally. I do believe I have found my answer with the Holy Spirit as my guide because I never looked at it from this perspective. It's not what you give but how you give. Surely, the church would like a tenth, but that may not be possible for some and that's my personal assumption based on people's ability to give. Samuel Dickey Gordon wrote the following:

> *I will never forget my mother's concise paraphrase of Malachi 3:10. The actual Bible text begins with the words "Bring the whole tithe into the storehouse" and ends with "I will...pour out blessing that." In effect, "you will be embarrassed over your lack of space to receive it." But my mother's paraphrase was this: "Give all He ask and take all He promised."*

Let your love for God show by your willingness to give and help the Church meet its needs. When we accepted Jesus Christ as our Lord and Savior, we agreed to do what it takes to ensure the smooth operation of the Church.

The Second Table

We, the chosen of God, have been taught that the Summary of the Decalogue is the Ten Commandments rolled into one. We know that the Ten Commandments contain two parts known as the first and second tables. This is also true of the Summary. According to the summary, the first table is "Love the Lord thy God with all thy heart, all thy soul and with all thy mind." This first table covers the first four commandments of the Ten Commandments. They describe our duty to God. "Love thy neighbor as thy self" constitutes the second table. This table deals with our duty to ourselves and to one another. The second table covers the last six commandments. Their order is fitting because reverence for God should always come before self.

However, I believe that over the years we have come to look at the second table literally and give strict definitions to each commandment. We must learn to understand that even though the sentences in God's Word may be short, the meaning is far reaching and we must always seek the greater understanding.

Honor your Father and Mother: We are to respect our parents and be obedient. Sometimes this goes against the grain of our personality or thought process. But out of reverence to God who gave us this commandment, we are obligated to respect and obey. Matthew 10:37 reminds us that "Anyone who loves his father or mother more than me is not worthy of me." God is Supreme and spiritual, but in the natural order of human relationships, parents are supreme. In our earlier years when we are under their roof, to respect and obey was not so hard for the majority of us. As we grow older and set out on our own, we tend to forget several of the things they taught, did and sacrificed for us. We begin to talk back and disrespect them as if they were the child. I believe that the second part of this commandment should prevent us from reaching this point. "So that you may live long in the land the lord your God is giving you." It is apparent that this refers to the Land of Milk and Honey; however, God's word is timeless and applies today when it comes to our Father and Mother so that we may be blessed by God for being obedient. This is an obligation that we must hold too.

You shall not murder. We have come to think of this as a physical action. This is not the case. We must understand the full effect of this commandment in order to be in compliance with God's will. Matthew Henry says, "thou shalt not do anything hurtful or injurious to the health, ease, and life, of thy own body, or any other person's unjustly." This covers physical and mental aspects of human life. The tongue in this case plays a very important role when we discuss others in our conversations. If we don't like a person, character assignation is very easy. This commandment is inclusive of all humans. If a person commits suicide, they have violated this commandment simply by killing themselves and rightly fall under Henry's explanation of thy own body.

You shall not steal. We relate this to taking the property of another without permission or right, which includes secretly or by force. When grocery shopping, if you notice an item did not get rung up on your purchase and you do not inform the clerk, you are guilty of stealing. Additionally, if you change the price on an item to a lesser price, you are stealing because you did not pay the original price and knowingly deprived the store of revenue.

Obviously I did not include all six of the commandments in the Second Table. The point is to get each of us to understand that these six commandments are not tightly jammed into a little box with a simple understanding. God meant them to cover the things that happen in day to day living. Therefore their scope is enormous. If each of us examines these six commandants more closely, we will find several things we are doing that do not line up with the will of God. To bring it to someone's attention is one thing. If we personally do nothing to change our behavior, we are disobedient to God's word.

Sitting at the Master's Feet

To sit at the master's feet, to me, means to be an understudy of someone with great insight and knowledge. It can be applied to any undertaking that requires extensive study from a single instructor or authority on a subject of study or practice leading to proficiency.

I recently read a writing that talked about missionary work. It posed a very interesting question. How could they, the missionaries, do the work required of them and still spend time with God? They spent all their time doing the physical work of trying to spread God's word spiritually to others. Their days were long and their rest short. They became tired and in a sense wondered how they could keep up this pace while not being refreshed by the Word of God. "Sitting at the Master's Feet" is my understanding or explanation of what it takes for us to work and meet the demands of today's society and continue to have time for God and work in the vineyard.

Looking at the Apostles and understanding that they followed Jesus during his ministry for three years, we realize that Jesus spent this time teaching them as much as he could about the ways of God, how God operates, and what to expect from God. He did this through the accomplishment of miracles, teaching through parables, and during quiet time spent giving them instructions through the Holy Spirit in private. The things he taught them during these three years as understudies can be easily described as their "Sitting at the Master's Feet."

In Matthew Chapter 28, the angels instructed the women who went and found the tomb empty to go quickly to the disciples, give them the news of the risen Christ, and inform them that He was going ahead of them into Galilee. The eleven went to Galilee. The instructions they received were as a result of "Sitting at the Master's Feet".

In Acts 1:3 we are told, "After his suffering, he showed himself to these men and gave many convincing proofs that he was alive. He appeared to them over a period of forty days and spoke about the kingdom of God." This was another opportunity for the Apostles to sit at the master's feet and receive additional teachings He had not revealed to them before. He spoke to them on occasion about the Comforter; the gift His Father promised which resulted in them being baptized with the Holy Spirit.

My first statement was "To sit at the master's feet to me means to be an understudy of someone with great insight and knowledge." God is the master of all. He sits high and looks low. He is above all. So to sit at His feet is an understatement. Because of His omni-, there is nothing lacking in His teaching. Understanding of the Bible can only be accomplished by study and God's revealing of His words through the Holy Spirit. I do realize that God could just drop this knowledge in our head if that were His will. However, the study of God's word allows for grooming, leads to joy in knowing the Lord, and strengthens our faith. We learn that He is in control. The time those missionaries needed to spend with God and accomplish their work has a simple answer. Give your time to God first, by reading His word, praying, and being blessed by the Holy Spirit. You will find that God is able to make time stand still, or **so** it would appear to us as humans. The things we thought we did not have time to accomplish would be completed with time to spare. Sitting at the Master's Feet for me is simple. We must daily put Him first. Spend time praying, reading, and studying His word and all things which are according to His will can be accomplished in due time without worry or hassle. The spreading and teaching of His Word will become second nature because He will be in control. With God at the helm, all things are possible and flow smoothly. He always provides His children with whatever is required to accomplish His will, be it sleep or resources. Sit at the master's feet and let Him take control over your life.

The Journey is Too Much for Me

"The Journey is Too Much for Me" can be a multitude of endeavors. They can be of any length with respect to time or distance. The Journey I speak of is the Christian Journey. To live a life dedicated to the Lord is not as easy as one would think. Each person must be equipped with a set of character traits peculiar to them. Along with these character traits, we must show determination. We must at some time stop, or stand still, to be replenished by the strength that comes from God. Faith is a must.

On this Christian Journey, we encounter all types of obstacles. Our determination to complete the journey must prevail, and it will if we are guided by God's plans for our life. During this journey, we will be challenged, but we must recognize opposition as a way of strengthening our faith and service to God. As Christians we must realize that the more we do for God, the more Satan will try to derail us. Satan is in the business of winning souls for hell, while God is determined to bless us with eternal life. Job struggled with understanding his condition and situation, but I cannot help but think of Elihu, the young man who spoke up after listening to his elders. "God does all things to a man – twice, even three times – to turn back his soul from the pit, that the light of life may shine on him." God's purpose is always for good, and we must be determined to navigate the obstacles of life, realizing that we do not understand all God allows but must trust Him to bring us through the fiery furnace.

Just like any journey, especially if it's long, we get tired and need a break to rest, regain our strength and continue. We have the Church of Jesus Christ and the leading of the Holy Spirit as our refueling stations. We can get weekly food for our soul through regular attendance at Sunday services. During the week, we can get a tune-up from attendance at Bible Study or some other form of gospel experience that stresses the Word of

God. However, no Sunday service or weekly tune-up can replace the rest and strength we gain from our personal commitment to God's Word. This personal commitment of reading, studying, and praying allows the Holy Spirit to communicate with us directly and invigorate our mind, body and soul. Daily communion with God helps us to grow along our journey and prepares us for those obstacles that may get in our way. "Let us then approach the throne of grace with confidence, so that we may receive mercy and find grace to help us in our time of need," Hebrews 4:16.

Being sure of what we hope for and certain of what we do not see is faith, as described in Hebrew 11. Many examples are given in this chapter to help us understand that faith is what helps us complete the journey. Believing in Christ is only the beginning. We have to believe the Word of God without reservation. "Just because" is enough for me. Just because God said it in His Word is enough for me to accept what He promised. He did not promise me that this journey would be without trials and tribulations, but He did promise me that He would be beside me all the way. He knew that I would get weak and even sick on occasions. He knew that He would need to be there to console me and heal me physically and mentally. I realized that to live a Christian life is a journey that is too much for me and that I would need help. My help and strength comes from the Lord, and I am sure I will complete the journey and find rest in eternity with God's word as my guide. Christ promised that if I am not ashamed of Him and His message before man, He will not be ashamed of me before His Father in glory. Glory is where this journey leads me.

Bibliography

Carter, Thomas, ed. *Spurgeon's Commentary on Greatest Chapters of the Bible*. Grand Rapids: Kregel Publications, 1998.

Chamber, Oswald. *My Utmost for His Highest*. Grand Rapids: Discovery House Publishing, 1963.

Davis, Rebecca and Susan Mesner, eds. *The Treasury of Religious & Spiritual Quotations: Words to Live By.* The Stonesong Press, Inc., 1994.

Falwell, Jerry, ed. *Liberty Bible Commentary*. Nashville: Old-Time Gospel Hour, 1982.

Henry, Matthew. *Commentary on the Whole Bible*. Zondervan Publishing House, 1961.

Holy Bible, New International Version. Biblica, Inc., 1984.

Murray, Andrew. *God's Best Secrets*. Whitaker House, 1998.

The Life Application Study Bible, New International Version. Zondervan Publishing House, 2005.

Young, Sarah. *Jesus Calling*. Harper Collins, Inc., 2004.